Ovid

CLASSICAL WORLD SERIES

Aristophanes and his Theatre of the Absurd, Paul Cartledge
Art and the Romans, Anne Haward
Athens and Sparta, S. Todd
Athens under Tyrants, J. Smith
Athletics in the Ancient World, Zahra Newby
Attic Orators, Michael Edwards
Augustan Rome, Andrew Wallace-Hadrill
Cicero and the End of the Roman Republic, Thomas Wiedemann
Cities of Roman Italy, Guy de la Bédoyère
Classical Archaeology in the Field, S. J. Hill, L. Bowkett and
K. & D. Wardle
Classical Epic: Homer and Virgil, Richard Jenkyns
Democracy in Classical Athens, Christopher Carey
Early Greek Lawgivers, John Lewis
Environment and the Classical World, Patricia Jeskins
Greece and the Persians, John Sharwood Smith
Greek and Roman Historians, Timothy E. Duff
Greek and Roman Medicine, Helen King
Greek Architecture, R. Tomlinson
Greek Literature in the Roman Empire, Jason König
Greek Sculpture, Georgina Muskett
Greek Tragedy: An Introduction, Marion Baldock
Greek Vases, Elizabeth Moignard
Homer: The Iliad, William Allan
Julio-Claudian Emperors, T. Wiedemann
Lucretius and the Didactic Epic, Monica Gale
Morals and Values in Ancient Greece, John Ferguson
Mycenaean World, K. & D. Wardle
Plato's Republic and the Greek Enlightenment, Hugh Lawson-Trancred
Plays of Euripides, James Morwood
Plays of Sophocles, A. F. Garvie
Political Life in the City of Rome, J. R. Patterson

Religion and the Greeks, Robert Garland
Religion and the Romans, Ken Dowden
Roman Architecture, Martin Thorpe
The Roman Army, David Breeze
Roman Britain, S. J. Hill and S. Ireland
Roman Egypt, Livia Capponi
Roman Frontiers in Britain, David Breeze
The Roman Poetry of Love, Efi Spentzou
Slavery in Classical Greece, N. Fisher
Spectacle in the Roman World, Hazel Dodge
Studying Roman Law, Paul du Plessis

Also available from Bloomsbury

Ovid: Love Songs, Genevieve Liveley
Ovid's 'Metamorphoses', Genevieve Liveley
Ovid: Myth and Metamorphosis, Sarah Annes Brown
Ovid and His Love Poetry, Rebecca Armstrong

Ovid: A Poet on the Margins

Laurel Fulkerson

Bloomsbury Academic
An imprint of Bloomsbury Publishing Plc

B L O O M S B U R Y
LONDON · OXFORD · NEW YORK · NEW DELHI · SYDNEY

Bloomsbury Academic

An imprint of Bloomsbury Publishing Plc

50 Bedford Square	1385 Broadway
London	New York
WC1B 3DP	NY 10018
UK	USA

www.bloomsbury.com

BLOOMSBURY and the Diana logo are trademarks of Bloomsbury Publishing Plc

First published 2016

© Laurel Fulkerson, 2016

Laurel Fulkerson has asserted her right under the Copyright, Designs and Patents Act, 1988, to be identified as Author of this work.

British Library Cataloguing-in-Publication Data

A catalogue record for this book is available from the British Library.

ISBN:	PB:	978-1-47253-134-6
	ePDF:	978-1-47252-734-9
	ePub:	978-1-47252-317-4

Library of Congress Cataloging-in-Publication Data

A catalog record for this book is available from the Library of Congress.

Typeset by RefineCatch Limited, Bungay, Suffolk

To Bill Fulkerson and Kay Dundas, with thanks for a place in exile.

Contents

List of Illustrations   x
Preface   xi
Acknowledgements   xii
Abbreviations of Ovidian Works   xiii

1   Life on the Margins   1
    1.1 Truth Stranger than Fiction: Poet Exiled Under
         Suspicious Circumstances!   1
    1.2 Meanwhile, Back in Rome . . .: Ovid's Historical Context   18
2   Repetition-Compulsion and Ovidian Excess   29
    2.1 Now You See Him, Now You Still See Him:
         Ovidian Narrative Style and Metre   29
    2.2 Same Story, Different Day: Repetition and Reception   47
3   Romans at Home and Abroad: Identity and
    the Colonial Subject   59
    3.1 Strangers in a Strange Land: Explorers and Exiles   59
    3.2 Speaking and Silence: Victims and Victimizers   66
    3.3 Empire and Colonialism   80

Further Readings   89
Glossary of Proper Names and Latin Terms   93
Index   101

List of Illustrations

1: Map of the Roman Empire at the time of Ovid.   2

2: De Remedio Amoris (manuscript of *Ars Amatoria* 1).
© DEA PICTURE LIBRARY/Contributor.   10

3: Archaeological excavation site, mosaic of Pyramus and
Thisbe, Roman mythology, House of Dionysos,
Archäologischer Park Paphos © imageBROKER /
Alamy Stock Photo.   34

4: Attributed to a Dutch artist active in Rome Narcissus,
1640s. Oil on canvas, 45 x 56 3/8 inches, SN885.
Collection of The John and Mable Ringling Museum
of Art, the State Art Museum of Florida, Florida State
University.   37

5: Correggio, Jupiter and Io. © Heritage Images/
Contributor.   54

6: Cesari, Diana and Actaeon. © The Museum of Fine
Arts Budapest/Scala, Florence.   69

7: Rodin, Pygmalion and Galatea. © The Metropolitan
Museum of Art/Art Resource/Scala, Florence.   71

8: Houasse, Minerve et Arachne. © Heritage
Images/Contributor.   72

Preface

This study presents Ovid as a poet animated by a unified set of concerns throughout his long and prolific career, rather than as a man destroyed by circumstances. As such, it is a study of poetics much more than a biography. My goal in this volume has been to offer what I see as the most compelling interpretative tools for understanding Ovid. I am well aware that some of them, taken together, seem mutually contradictory, but I believe that the ambiguities can be reconciled. Above all, I hope to encourage all readers of this work to devote more of their energies to Ovid, who will richly reward any attention paid to him.

Working on the Ovidian oeuvre as a whole in the synoptic way required for this book has confirmed a long-held belief that Ovid is the ideal combination of fox and hedgehog: he has more than one good trick up his toga, but he repeats some of them an awful lot. Readers should be aware that I have tried to cover the most prevalent features of Ovidian style and poetics, such that nearly every example from Ovid's work could have been replaced with several others. I have tried to mix well-known passages with obscure ones, preferring those that allowed me to discuss more than one topic at a time. And, of course, a number of them are personal favourites. The *Metamorphoses* is by far Ovid's most famous work, and quite possibly his best; I have tried to balance this fact with the equally compelling imperative to introduce less familiar moments and characters to a wider audience.

In keeping with the aims of this series, the Further Readings section bears the scantiest possible testimony to the richness and variety of excellent work being done on Ovid. I hereby apologize to all who feel slighted by my omissions, which are enormous. Translations are mine, with the hope of capturing a small portion of what is so marvellous about Ovid's Latin.

Acknowledgements

My first debt of gratitude is to Mark Petrini, under whose tutelage I began reading Ovid, and my second to Gareth D. Williams, for nurturing my Ovidianism, and providing encouragement and structure for this project at its early stages. Thanks are due too to several readers of earlier drafts: Jessica H. Clark, Megan Drinkwater, W. Jeffrey Tatum and Gareth D. Williams, and to the graduate students in my *Metamorphoses* seminar at FSU in the spring of 2013, who were the first auditors of my nascent thoughts and who, with their extremely varied interests, made me aware of just how much Ovid has to offer. My scholarly debts and influences will probably be obvious to professionals; interested amateurs will find some hints in the Further Readings section. I thank too my students Andrew Ficklin and Bart Natoli for written work and discussions which have helped me to frame my thoughts on Germanicus's triumph and on Ovidian silences (the latter now a Texas dissertation, 'Speech, Community, and the Formation of Memory in the Ovidian Exilic Corpus', 2014). The dedication reflects a personal obligation, but also my hope that, finally, I have written something that normal people might enjoy reading.

Abbreviations of Ovidian Works

Amores – Am.: Loves

Ars Amatoria – Ars: The Art of Loving

Epistulae Ex Ponto – EP: Letters from the Black Sea

Fasti – Fas.: Roman Calendar

Heroides – Her.: (Letters from) Heroines

Ibis – Ib.: Curses

Medicamina Facei Feminae – MF: Potions for Female Beauty

Metamorphoses – Met.: Changes

Remedia Amoris – RA: Remedies for Love

Tristia – Tr.: Sad Poems

Life on the Margins

1.1 Truth Stranger than Fiction: Poet Exiled Under Suspicious Circumstances!

Let us begin at the end. This particular end is cold, and far from Rome; indeed, it is located 'at the outer perimeter of the unknown world' (*Tr.* 3.3.3). The place, Tomis, in the Roman province of Pontus (see Fig. 1), is where the barbarians live, and a sophisticated Roman poet like Publius Ovidius Naso, known to us as Ovid, has no business being here. Tomis, now on the map as Constanța in Romania (it was originally a colony of the Greek city Miletus, founded in the sixth century BCE, and features a statue of the poet in Ovid Square), is the proper place to start because doing so enables us to adopt a unique perspective on the life, and especially the work, of the dazzling and puzzling poet Ovid. For nearly all readers come to Ovid's poetry knowing about his unseemly fall from grace, a spectacular, Icarus-like descent from which he seems never to have recovered. Ovid, darling of the glittering world of Roman literary culture, was forced to finish out his life in the middle of nowhere. He was relegated by the emperor Augustus in the year 8 CE for two causes, as he tells us himself, with apparent frankness, *carmen et error*, a poem and a mistake (*Tr.* 2.207). The poem, almost certainly, was the *Ars Amatoria*, which could certainly be understood, and not only by a grumpy old man, as encouraging adultery.

About the *error* Ovid is resolutely silent, if your definition of silence is broad enough to include constant allusion, picking at the scab of the offence with a consistency that ensures it can never be far from readers' minds. We never do learn what happened, though many historians and

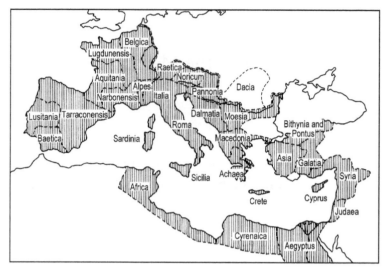

Fig. 1 Map of the Roman Empire at the time of Ovid.

novelists have put together the intriguing hints in a variety of ways, some connecting the relegation to political scheming, some to adultery with imperial women, and some to a combination of the two. Or perhaps, along the lines of his own mythic hero Actaeon (see Section 2.1), Ovid saw Augustus's wife Livia in the bath? We may never know, but we have already stumbled upon a key characteristic of Ovid's poetry, that of ambiguity, or perhaps paradox. For Ovid gives contradictory information about what he did (or saw), about Augustus's reaction to it, and about his own later understanding of the gravity of the event. Individual readers can come up with many different scenarios – and this is true of a great many aspects of Ovid's poetry, including what to make of his exilic work, which might be understood as an attempt at apology and reparation, or a sober rejection of all of his previous work, or a cheeky thumbing of the nose at the emperor.

Indeed, this silence-which-speaks is perhaps the most salient fact about Ovid's later literary career: if the relegation was intended to shut him up, it failed spectacularly. He continued to write, ten books of poetry at least (five of the *Tristia*, four of the *Epistulae Ex Ponto*, and the

Ibis), and to rewrite what had already been written: we are told, again by Ovid (first at *Tr.* 1.7.27–8 and sporadically thereafter) that he revised the fifteen books of the *Metamorphoses*, and the *Fasti* bear signs of revision after the death of Augustus (see Section 2.2 on Ovid's career-long habit of returning to previous work). Most readers cannot refuse the temptation to read backward, to look for clues in these earlier works that will unlock the mystery of What Really Happened, especially in such memorable scenes as that of *Met.* 6, when the goddess Athena nearly beats to death her human rival Arachne, for losing a weaving contest with her (see Section 2.2). Or perhaps, for *not* losing the contest: the narrative is notoriously inconclusive, and gods in Ovid have a habit of being sore losers.

Such readerly detective work reflects Ovid's own keen interest in how, and by whom, stories are told, and his near-obsessive return to certain stories and mythic patterns throughout his poetry. Among the stories he finds most compelling are those which focus on aberrant behaviour and its aftermath, and on the exploitation of power differentials. So the lenses of exile and otherness, on the one hand, and of revision and repetition on the other, will serve us throughout this work as structural metaphors, offered in different combinations for different purposes. Some of the questions raised by this juxtaposition of approaches include the following (but this list is certainly not intended to preclude other possibilities): If you have written yourself into exile, can you (re-)write yourself out? If a work reflects its author, does revision entail a change of heart? Is the poet-who-revises the 'same person' as the poet-who-wrote? Should we understand Ovid's lifelong revisions as a kind of repetition-compulsion? How can we tell the difference between the 'same story' and a different story? How do we read the literally alienated stance Ovid presents in the poetry from exile in light of the figurative alienation discernible across all of his work?

In this section, we sketch the sweep of Ovid's literary output, and then focus a bit more closely on individual poems. There is much controversy about the dating of Ovid's works, especially the earlier ones, in part because of his habit of modifying published collections.

Table 1 gives the generally agreed-upon chronology (and includes a few other key dates in Roman history).

Even these outlines, broad as they are, remain difficult to narrow. This is in the main because from his very first extant work, Ovid depicts himself as willing to engage in audacious generic experiments. He repeats himself endlessly, and with ingeniously endless variation, both

Table 1 Ovidian chronology.

Event	Date
Ovid's birth	20 March 43 BCE
Battle of Actium	31 BCE
Octavian given the title of Augustus	27 BCE
First (five-book) edition of the *Amores*	After 20 BCE?
Heroides 1–15 (the 'single' *Heroides*)	In between two editions of the *Amores* (sometimes dated earlier)
Death of Vergil (and public release of *Aeneid*)	19 BCE
Saecular Games celebrated at Rome	17 BCE
Medea (a lost tragedy)	Some time after the *Heroides*
Second (three-book) edition of the *Amores*	Some time between 7 BCE and 1 CE
Augustus named 'father of the fatherland' (*pater patriae*)	2 BCE
Ars Amatoria, Books 1–2 (and 3?)	2 BCE
Remedia Amoris (and *Ars* 3?)	2 CE
Medicamina Faciei Feminae	Some time before 8 CE?
Metamorphoses	Written 2–8 CE, not clear when published
Fasti	Written 2–8 CE, not clear when published
Ovid relegated to Tomis	8 CE
Tristia	9–12 CE
Heroides 16–21 (the 'double' *Heroides*)	Some time after 8 CE
Ibis	10–12 CE?
Epistulae Ex Ponto	13–16 CE
Phaenomena (translation of Aratus's poem)	??
Ovid's death	*c.* 17 CE

There are also a number of works traditionally attributed to Ovid which are probably not by the poet: the *Halieutica*, the *Nux* and the *Consolatio ad Liviam*.

in terms of the topics and themes he chooses to treat, and in the larger structures of his work, which constantly reinvent themselves and offer second thoughts about only *apparently* completed poems. 'Variations upon a theme' are a noticeable feature of the Ovidian oeuvre even given that he wrote in a time when many gifted writers of both prose and poetry were creating new and hybrid forms of literature.

Like all Roman authors, Ovid models himself upon predecessors (the epic poet Vergil, author of the instantly classic *Aeneid*, is probably the most important of an exceedingly long list of Greek and Latin authors), but he also strikes out boldly on his own. His first extant poetic statement, expressed in the preface to the second edition of the *Amores*, provides a characteristic self-assessment (*Am. pr.* 1–4): 'We who were recently the five poetry books of Naso are now three – the author liked it this way better than that. And although there may still be no pleasure for you once you have read them, at least your punishment will be lessened by two books.'

This is not, however successful the first edition had been, a statement you would expect from such a young author. To begin with, Ovid asserts the superiority of his own judgement (*you* may have liked the first edition, but Ovid knows better), and then undermines his claim by promising that, however tiresome his poetry is, at least there is now less of it to get through. The processes of editing and of writing are different, even though an author normally does both, and the preface of the *Amores* shows a quintessentially Ovidian split in personae, whereby the pretensions of one overconfident character are undermined by a different narrative voice, which also soon proves to be problematic. These words also provide us with the perfect introduction to the kinds of issues we will regularly face in attempting to understand Ovidian poetics, which are manifold in nature. Ovid is the poet who has such a firm grasp on his craft that he can undermine his own work, 'banishing' two of his own books because they no longer please him, the con artist who assures us that we will be safer if we remember not to trust him, the ruthless exploiter of women who nonetheless depicts them with remarkable sensitivity. Indeed, for a modern audience, Ovid has become both a byword for the kind of frivolity that only rarely coincides with a truly great talent (Oscar Wilde offers a good comparison, or any number of outrageous but extremely talented contemporary professional athletes or musicians), and an early martyr for those interested in tracing the history of political oppression. Each of these stereotypes is, of course, only part of the Ovidian story, but each contains a grain of the truth.

Not surprisingly, all of the most common ways in which Ovid has been read over the past two thousand years can be supported by his poetry. We will touch upon many of these in the pages that follow, but for now it is sufficient to note that all of Ovid's poetry, in different ways, frustrates the reader's desire to know where to stand, through a series of unreliable narrators, stories which change mid-stream, and deceptive surfaces which imperfectly reveal underlying realities (or perhaps merely another surface). In this, and many other ways, Ovid is both a poet of his own time and of ours. The tales of the *Metamorphoses* are perhaps the clearest instances of this complex poetic practice, but another useful example comes from a pair of poems in the *Amores*, 2.7 and 8, to which we shall return repeatedly. The first poem reassures Ovid's jealous girlfriend Corinna that she has nothing to fear from her hairdresser/slave Cypassis; Ovid is annoyed by Corinna's refusal to trust him, and assures her that if he were interested in cheating on her – which of course he isn't – it would never be with a slave, especially one so loyal to her mistress! The second poem, in a deft reversal, warns Cypassis, with whom Ovid has in fact had an affair, to be more discreet in the future, disavows his earlier dismissal of slaves as unattractive, and threatens her with exposure if she does not continue sleeping with him.

In addition to the way these poems undermine any sympathy we might have had for the narrator, they show Ovid's fascination with *ars* ('art', but also 'technique'; the arrangement of female beauty, after all, is the subject of Ovid's own fragmentary *Medicamina Faciei Feminae*). They also create an in-group and an out-group. Ovid's world contains masters, usually male, in a position of superiority even when (or because) they are willing to forego enforcing their authority, and the rest: women, slaves, monsters, and barbarians, who may come out on top once in a while, mostly in the interest of narrative variation. Contrary to what we might expect, Ovid manages to occupy in his own narrative personae both of these positions; by birth a dominating force, he assumes a position of subordination with such skill and ease that it is easy to become confused. But, while Ovid does play with the poetic theme of *servitium amoris* (the conceit that love is a kind of slavery, and the lover is 'enslaved' to his mistress – a precise reversal of the likely power dimensions of the real-life analogue to the elegiac relationship), he does so less than other elegists, preferring to embody other subservient roles.

The Poems

The next section will trace out some of the essential characteristics of Ovid's Rome. For now, we focus on chronicling his literary output. In the last years of the millennium, he was at the top of his game, riding high on the successes of his elegiac poems (see Section 2.1 on elegy): first, the *Amores*, which, deliberately or not, put the capstone on the genre for generations to come by pushing its boundaries to their utmost. Like other collections of elegiac poetry, it featured a single mistress as the object of the lover's affections (Corinna), but it innovated in not actually introducing her to readers until the fifth poem; the first four focus on Ovid himself, and detail the process by which he came to write poetry – and Ovid regularly returns to such metapoetic gestures throughout the *Amores*, as in 3.1 when he stages a debate about his career plans between the goddesses Elegy and Tragedy, or in 2.18 when he 'advertises' other works. The *Amores* also transform elegy by treating themes related to the elegiac lifestyle, but avoided by other elegists, perhaps because they were 'too real': unwanted pregnancy and abortion (2.13–14), impotence (3.7), juggling two mistresses at once (2.10), and even mention of his wife (3.13).

The 'single' *Heroides*, letters written in the persona of well-known mythological women, seem to have come next, applying elegiac metaphors and worldviews to mythological characters (the women, for instance, describe themselves as *puellae*, the word used of elegiac mistresses). Like the *Amores*, this collection is also a bold departure from predecessors, suggesting that the world of elegy has the potential to consume everything. Use of examples taken from myth was nothing new, but Ovid translates the characters so literally into his own world that they become hybrids of fact and fiction. And they prefigure Ovid's use of myth and character study, later in the *Ars Amatoria*, *Metamorphoses* and *Fasti*. But the *Heroides* are also interesting in their own right, as they show Ovid's gift at creating plausible inner lives for fictional characters; for instance, *Heroides* 8 speculates about the psychology of Hermione, and paints a compelling, and otherwise unexamined, picture of what it might be like to be the (neglected) daughter of Helen, the most beautiful woman in the world. For many readers the poems are depressing, as their heroines write into a vacuum, never receiving a response from the men they address, and never effecting any change in their worlds. This is, however, not the only way of reading them (see Section 2.1). Ovid's excursus into mythological fiction was, during certain time periods, his most influential work, and the *Heroides* are now enjoying a revival. There was also the extremely successful tragedy *Medea* (we have two fragments, rave reviews from later generations, and a Senecan version which must allude to it).

Soon after followed the didactic (i.e., instructional – at least nominally) *Ars Amatoria* and *Remedia Amoris* (see Fig. 2). These demonstrated that if Ovid could 'kill' elegy, he could also resurrect it in new forms, and that he excelled in the contemporary poets' game of putting uncongenial topics to verse. Vergil's *Georgics* (a poem offering instruction about the farming life) is the obvious precursor to these poems, but Ovid draws style and even material from many others, from Nicander's *Theriaca* and *Alexipharmaca*, on animal bites and poisons, to Lucretius's *De Rerum Natura*, a six-book exposition of Epicurean philosophy and science. The *Ars* – whose subject is love – is, of course, a joke: nobody *learns* how to fall in love: it just happens. But also, if anyone did want instruction, how could a poem possibly help? Finally, the *kind* of love here being taught, elegiac, is not the sort any sane person would want to learn, as it entails a miserable way of life. The parodic nature of the *Ars*, in fact, gets at the very heart of the didactic tradition – for Vergil's *Georgics* are also not a straightforward manual to farming, and putting knowledge in poetic metres makes sense only in an oral tradition, to aid memory: a prose handbook, or, indeed, apprenticeship to an expert, would work better for most of the topics set to verse. *Ars* 1 focuses on teaching men how to choose and obtain the woman they want (literally, the one to whom you will say 'you are the only one for me', *Ars* 1.42, but this monogamy is serial at best); *Ars* 2 continues by explaining how to keep the relationship going (repeating itself, since you behave in more or less the same ways to keep the girl as you did to win her). Then, with no earlier hint that this was in the offing, *Ars* 3 addresses itself to women, advising them on how to keep up their end of the relationship (see Section 3.2 on one of the major differences between the instructions given to women and to men). And once more Ovid defies expectations, for the *Remedia Amoris*, which seems to have been published separately, but might also be read as 'volume four', begins from the premise that for some, the elegiac way of love might be dangerous, or even fatal. The instructor had sprinkled throughout earlier books warnings about these hazards, mostly centring on the point that although elegy requires systemic falsification and pretence, it can still engender real emotions, which hurt. So the *Remedia* help the (male, but perhaps also female) lover to get out. They offer only a temporary remedy, however, as one of the poem's most consistent suggestions is to find a replacement woman and start over (presumably, with *Ars* 1). Later authors also provide us with a few fragments of Ovid's translation of Aratus's *Phainomena*, an erudite Hellenistic didactic poem about constellations, translated also by Cicero, and by Augustus's adoptive son Germanicus.

It is not clear what prompted the switch, but Ovid's masterpiece, the fifteen-book *Metamorphoses,* moves to the metre of dactylic hexameters (in which epic poetry was written; see Section 2.1). It tells stories of 'forms changed into new bodies' (*Met.* 1.1–2), beginning with the creation of the world, and ending with the poet's claim to immortality

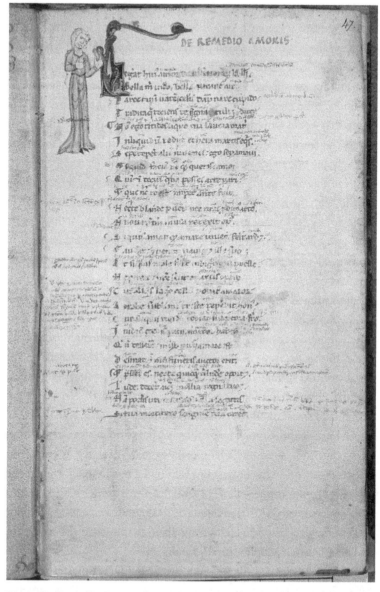

Fig. 2 De Remedio Amoris (manuscript of *Ars Amatoria* 1).

'in whatever parts of the conquered world Roman power extends' (*Met.* 15.877), ranging over a vast array of material set in widely spaced geographical areas. Its breadth of subject matter makes the poem unlike typical epic poetry, as does its tone: epic normally tells just one story, for instance, of the return home of Odysseus after the Trojan War – although even there, inset narratives, prophecies and foreshadowing make the structure complex. The *Metamorphoses*, by contrast, covers everything, and does so in a chaotic jumble. Its structure is roughly chronological: the first five books detail the activities of the gods and demigods; the second five focus on mythical heroes; the last five are 'historical', although for Romans the boundaries between early history and myth are permeable. Spatially, the poem also covers a lot of ground, moving from the primordial ooze, through Greece, by way of a number of 'exotic' eastern locales, to Rome and finally, to the heavens themselves, when Julius Caesar becomes a god and Augustus is about to. So too, the way Ovid tells his stories is eclectic: the *Metamorphoses* is a composite poem, combining gods, cosmogonies, historical events, aetiologies and battles (epic material) with elegiac love stories, narratives that would be comfortable in pastoral poetry, tales from the Greek and Roman tragic and comic stages, folklore motifs (familiar to a Roman audience from mime performances) and a series of excursuses on philosophical topics, in a format that bears remarkable affinities to the 'universal history' being written by contemporaries. The overall effect of this conglomeration of genres is to embody confusion: the poem, like so much of Ovid's work, is not quite any one thing, and a reader has just started putting interpretative clues together in one way when conflicting evidence intrudes.

Each of Ovid's stories in the *Metamorphoses*, at least nominally, coheres to the overall theme of metamorphosis, and so nearly all of them involve a physical change. Most often this change comes at the end, and it can clarify what had earlier been implicit, as in the case of Lycaon (= wolf-man), the first person-to-animal metamorphosis in *Met.* 1; his predatory and cruel inner nature ultimately becomes apparent as he literally becomes a wolf. Or metamorphosis explains how something came to be the way it is (such as in *Met.* 4 why the sunflower always faces the sun – she was a woman named Clytie, loved but then spurned by the sun). But sometimes the causal relation is obscure (Callisto, the daughter of Lycaon, displays no ursine tendencies, besides spending time in the forest, before she is changed into a bear in *Met.* 2). While metamorphosis often provides a conclusion to the story, sometimes it is patently tacked-on: the long and engrossing tale of Phaethon's unfortunate ride on the chariot of the sun (his father) ends in *Met.* 2 with much of the world burned up, and Phaethon himself in ashes (a metamorphosis, but not a very satisfying one) – but then, as if Ovid worried we might think he was cheating, he explains that Phaethon's sisters mourned for him so much that they were turned into trees which secrete amber, as a permanent record of their tears. The poem's descriptions of physical change also vary, but there is usually a telling detail, or a focus on the precise moment when one thing ceases to be itself and becomes another, as in *Met.* 1 when the nymph Daphne (= bay tree), having prayed to escape the clutches of an amorous Apollo, feels 'her soft sides covered in thin bark, her hair growing into leaves, and her arms into branches; her foot, once so swift, clings in deep roots, and the treetops have her head' (1.549–51).

Over the course of the poem, Ovid incorporates over 250 metamorphoses: at several points there are multiple embedded narratives (i.e., a character tells a tale in which another person tells a tale), and Ovid eventually covers just about every situation in which one might relate a story (to gain love, to console oneself for a loss, to win a contest, to persuade the gods to give one's dead wife back, to teach a lesson, to obtain something from someone, to threaten, to entertain one's host or guest, to pass the time . . .). And many of Ovid's narrators, especially in the *Metamorphoses*, fail to achieve their aims. While it is difficult to summarize the themes of the poem, two of its regularly recurring topics are how change works, and how narrative works. Beyond this, the poem is full of really good stories: in terms of literary, artistic and musical responses to specific episodes, the *Metamorphoses* is arguably the most influential work of Western literature after the

Bible (all of the artworks illustrated in this volume depict stories from the *Metamorphoses*).

Concurrently with the *Metamorphoses*, Ovid is likely to have been working on the *Fasti*, a melding of historical and mythic tales (normally without metamorphosis) focusing on important events in the Roman year, in chronological, calendrical format. The *Fasti* is perhaps best known as a handbook of Roman religion, as the *Metamorphoses* is a handbook of myth, although each of these designations is misleading, given that Ovid is an active manipulator of received tradition, rather than a passive vehicle for it. We might therefore characterize his approach to both myth and religion as burlesque rather than chronicle; he is always more interested in what he can make of a story than in the story itself. The *Fasti* is also notorious because, although Ovid claims to have written twelve books, we have only six (*sex ... totidemque, Tr.* 2.549, see Section 3.1). The final six might, of course, have been lost, but many critics, noting the proliferation of Augustan themes in the latter half of the Roman year (not least the months of July and August, named after Augustus's adoptive father Julius Caesar and himself), are suspicious about whether they ever existed. And the *Fasti* itself bears unmistakable traces of revision, including two dedications, at the start of Books 1 and 2, to different members of the imperial family, which suggests that Ovid might have had the opportunity to finish the final volumes if he had wanted to. On the other hand, Ovid is regularly deceptive about his own work: in *Tr.* 1.7.27–8, he claims that the *Metamorphoses* was significantly less complete than the version we have suggests. Some scholars see closural elements in the sixth book of the *Fasti*, others do not. The *Fasti* is in some ways the most difficult of Ovid's works: it seems to require specialized knowledge of Roman history and religion. But in many ways it is also Ovid's most ambitious work, and it is certainly his most 'Roman'.

Ovid's later works were written during his exile from 8 CE, when he, the most famous living Roman poet, was relegated by the emperor Augustus to Tomis, located on the Black Sea. He continued to write poetry for another nine years or so, presumably until his death. There are five books of *Tristia* ('sad poems'), the first of which details his departure from Rome and first impressions of Tomis. The second book, a single poem, is in the form of an 'open letter' to Augustus, defending the poet and especially the *Ars Amatoria*, which he tells us was partly responsible for the relegation. In it, Ovid offers a lopsided reading of Greco-Roman literary history, and also questions (what he presents as) the emperor's assumption that poetry can lead to immoral behaviour. This is, as Ovid well knows, a catch-22, for if poetry has no effect on real life, then his letter to Augustus is pointless. On the other hand, if Augustus is tempted to relent based on his reading of *Tristia* 2, then Ovid's alibi is invalid, because he really could have encouraged adultery through his earlier poetry (see Section 3.3 for more on Ovid and Augustus). *Tristia* 3–5 treat a variety of themes as the poet settles in to his new life, focusing especially on his friends, the city of Rome, the anger of 'Jupiter' (= Augustus), and the unpleasantness of life at Tomis. It is during these years that Ovid also wrote the *Ibis*, an elegiac poem of invective against an enemy (given the pseudonym Ibis based on a poem of the same name by Callimachus), detailing all of the horrible ways in which he might suffer, drawn from mythology but also history. These include mutilation, starvation, torture, incest and cannibalism, among other things. The poem is excessively erudite – we can decipher only a portion of the stories Ovid alludes to – and has been read as a document of slipping sanity, but also as an exercise in humorous overstatement (for Ovid claims at line 641 of the poem that he has written 'only a little', and that he will write much more, if Ibis does not begin to behave himself!).

The double *Heroides* are also, for stylistic reasons, usually dated to these years. They are like the single letters in that they feature mythological love stories, but here the letters are paired: in each, a man writes to a woman, and the woman writes back; generally the man is interested in furthering the relationship and the woman is, at least on the surface, more hesitant. This situation offers a fundamental difference from the single letters, as communication is no longer fruitless. Including responses to letters enables Ovid to use irony on a new level, for one letter of a pair can pick up on themes latent in the other. It also bears out one of the claims of the teacher in the *Ars Amatoria*, that all women will eventually write back if you correspond with them often enough (*Ars* 1.483–6), and mirrors Ovid's exilic obsession with whether his friends will write back.

The *Epistulae Ex Ponto* are our last work from Ovid. In some ways they are like the *Tristia*, with the difference that they now no longer fear to name their addressees (*EP* 1.1.18). They concentrate more of their energies on the imperial family, including panegyrics (formal poems of praise), and many readers see them as reflecting the poet's gradual adaptation to his new life. They are also among the world's earliest colonial literature, written from the point of view of the ruler class about its 'barbarous' subjects (see Section 3.3).

It has never been quite clear to scholars what to make of the *Tristia* and *Epistulae Ex Ponto*. For some, they are self-evidently sincere outpourings, expressing the real man's genuine wishes to return home. Others point to the fact that Ovid's descriptions of Tomis owe much to earlier ethnographic literature describing 'wild places', and that his much-emphasized 'pose of decline' is nowhere apparent in the poetry itself, except perhaps in (what he himself admits is) a somewhat monotonous subject matter. Intent is difficult to discern: presumably, the biographical Ovid would have been very happy to receive permission to live somewhere less remote (a request he makes with tedious frequency). On the other hand, the exile poetry repeats many of the same sly and self-undermining gestures that we find in his earlier poetry, which makes it hard to decide if its requests should be taken at face value. So too, his treatment of the imperial family is hard to pin down: at *Tr.* 2.161–4, Ovid wishes that Livia will remain with Augustus for a long time, saying that she is 'worthy of no husband but you, and but for her, you would have been suited for an unmarried life, and there was no other for you to marry'. Quite possibly this is simply a compliment about how well-suited the imperial couple are, but suspicious souls point out that both were previously married, and that Augustus forced an extremely pregnant Livia to marry him (such that

Livia was falsely known as a *univira*, 'one-man woman'), and that Augustus's own legislation (see Section 1.2) had denied the choice of an unmarried life to men of the upper classes. Beyond this, it is surely not wholly flattering to tell anyone that they could not possibly have found another marriage partner. Even passages of direct praise raise a flag for some readers, who consider it obvious that Ovid could have nothing positive to say about the man who caused his misery; for such readers every word is laden with irony. Others see these passages as genuine attempts to make amends, which read awkwardly to moderns with ideological leanings against one-person rule, or because the genre of imperial panegyric was still in its infancy, and its rules had yet to be determined. This is one of the many issues that remain unresolved about our poet (see Section 3.3); Ovid's poetry as a whole seems to seek a sophisticated, multi-valent response, such that nearly any conclusion drawn by one reader can be refuted with evidence gathered by another. But this, far from being a problem, means that repeated readings are richly repaid.

The exile poetry shows a number of distinct differences from Ovid's earlier work, but also combines earlier themes and habits in new ways. First, he writes *in propria persona*, as himself, which he had not done since his earliest work; so too, his troubled relationship to his exilic Muse is reminiscent in many ways of his relationship with Corinna, girlfriend of the *Amores*: Ovid is on the outside, wanting to get back in. Second, he returns to the letter-form of the *Heroides*. Third, the 'double-vision' that many see in the exile poetry is quintessentially Ovidian, as is the characteristic blending of fact with fiction (Ovid suggests that he himself can provide the *Metamorphoses* with a new ending, as he has changed from living to half-dead, *Tr.* 1.1.119–20, and he even writes a new preface, about his exile, *Tr.* 1.7.33–40). Finally, Ovid's portrayal of the world of Tomis as a militarized zone places him literally in the middle of the soldier's world he had invoked-but-avoided in a lifetime of poetry (*Am.* 1.9 expands at length upon the metaphor of love-as-war). The 'monotony' of the exile poetry is not wildly different from the monotony of the narrowly-circumscribed world of elegy. Most readers will find sex a more interesting topic than exile, but that is perhaps merely our prejudice.

Those interested in Ovid's life usually begin with *Tr.* 4.10, the poet's 'autobiography', written in the form of a defence speech, which mentions, among other things, his status as an Italian provincial equestrian ('knight'; this was the second-highest property class in Rome, and will have meant that the poet was wealthier than the vast majority of Romans – this is also the class from which Augustan poets tend to come), his three marriages, his brother – born exactly one year before Ovid – his family's career ambitions for him, and his uncanny ability to turn out polished verse unwittingly ('of its own will poetry came to me in suitable metre, and what I was trying to write became verse', *Tr.* 4.10.25–6). While it might be only the last statement that raises an eyebrow, many readers take the entire poem with a pinch of salt; in general, ancient biographies of poets – even their autobiographies – tell a story that seems appropriate or convenient to a specific purpose rather than one that is strictly true (so, for instance, this narrative hints that Ovid's personal life compares favourably to Augustus's, and suggests parallels also to the poet Catullus).

It is also worth noting the interesting fact that we have no independent contemporary attestation of the poet's exile. This is symbolic of the kinds of problems one always faces with Ovid, who regularly dances around the troubled boundaries between truth and fiction. As an example of the difficulties, take the poet's descriptions of Tomis. Ovid characterizes it as barbaric (i.e., nobody speaks Latin), and complains about the bitter cold, the lack of culture and the peculiar customs, dress and food of the locals. One of the highlights is the description in *Tr.* 3.10 of how the Getae must saw off their frozen wine each day; this vivid vignette emphasizes Ovid's isolation precisely by its near-normality (even here they drink wine, but how peculiarly!). In some ways, Ovid's descriptions resemble other ancient ethnographic narratives (dating back in the Greek world to the sixth century BCE), not least in their emphasis on foreign ways, but in other ways they are radically different. Tomis itself was an urban centre and probably almost nothing like Ovid describes it (it is now a resort town).

In much the same way as Ovidians are hesitant to use the exile poetry as a source about life in first-century CE Tomis, there is a growing realization that the *Amores* are similarly suspect as a transparently autobiographical record of a real-life extramarital affair (or even a composite series of affairs). Ovid's poetry always has a complex relationship to reality, especially when he claims to represent it faithfully. What – as we shall see – had once been a witty trope in Ovid's poetry, wherein the quintessential insider experimented with different aberrant and underprivileged personae, became finally more than a metaphor. It is almost too good, or too horrible, to be true that so Roman a poet ended his life on the margins of the empire.

1.2 Meanwhile, Back in Rome . . .: Ovid's Historical Context

Augustan Rome

At the end of his life, Ovid was an outsider, looking yearningly at Rome. He had always proclaimed himself a creature of the city (*Ars* 1.55–6, quoted at the end of this section), so he may have found this marginal position especially upsetting. We noted briefly earlier that Ovid's exilic self-portrait as a man longing for home has much in common with the ways the poet/lover in the earliest of Ovid's works, and, indeed, in Latin love elegy as a whole, positions himself as excluded from his girlfriend's embrace, and often from her front door as well. We shall see much more of the *puella* ('girl'), the maddening but maddeningly desirable object of elegiac love poetry; for now we note merely that portions of the exile poetry position Augustus himself in her role: the emperor and his city become the unattainable objects of Ovid's affections. But this amusing juxtaposition does not mean that Ovid's exile poetry is reducible to a joke – still less that we should take it entirely seriously. The relegated Ovid seems to be giving vent to authentic feelings of loss and, simultaneously, engaging in an elaborate and extended allusion to the genre he had made his own. While this blurring between fact and fiction may seem odd, it is a technique we see displayed throughout Ovid's works.

This metaphorical treatment of Augustus as *puella* raises a perennial question of Ovidian scholarship, namely, whether the poet is pro- or anti-Augustan. The topic was, as we shall see, very much in the air for contemporaries. But put in these terms, the question is unanswerable, not least because 'Augustanism' was not a monolithic entity; it seems rather to have entailed a series of individual negotiations and steps, tending toward certain goals. But its principles were probably never articulated clearly enough to allow an opposing platform to be created. 'Anti-Augustan' would simply mean against the man himself, and while it is certainly possible to see specific passages of Ovid's own work as deliberate attempts to annoy, embarrass or even nurture hostility against the emperor, this is not the only way of reading the poetry; the catch-22 we saw at the heart of *Tristia* 2 works both ways, so as to embroil both Ovid and Augustus in the work of figuring out what Ovid's love poetry, or Rome itself, actually means.

Rather than concentrating on Ovid's relationship to Augustanism, this section focuses on the time and place in which Ovid wrote, and especially on the instabilities inherent in living at the border between Republic and Empire (he was twelve years old when the battle of Actium was fought), at a time when nobody quite knew what would happen next. Although the start of the Roman Empire seems inevitable to us, for contemporaries it must have been anything but obvious. The late Republic had been marked by a series of civil wars, increasing violence and violation of traditional forms, and military warlords intent only upon increasing their own power, ideally through legal authority, but, at a last resort, through force. It is difficult to know, but reasonable to speculate, that most Romans were exhausted by the generation-long upheaval, and willing to give up some of what we might think of as their freedoms in order to regain a modicum of stability. This will be especially true among those of the lower classes, who had never expected to have much say in governance anyway. But among the upper classes, things may have been rather different: the men of the senate had been used to giving orders, not taking them, and one of the most serious problems facing early emperors was how to enable them to feel as if they continued to rule, without giving them too much real power.

Ovid's own lifetime coincided with the end of the Roman Republic, and, after a childhood in the turbulent thirties BCE, his adult years would have been spent in a world in which Augustus was the only real choice. We can see some evidence of this in the fact that, unlike that of his slightly older contemporaries, Vergil, Propertius and Horace, Ovid's poetry presents no surface anxiety about the fundamental nature of Rome, no worries about the future. If anything, he breezily underestimates the difficulties and problems inherent in (re-)stabilizing Rome and its dominions (see Section 3.3). The transition from Republic to Empire brought with it a wide variety of changes, and reactions to them, which we can see reflected in the literature and art dating to just before Ovid's time, but our poet's work looks forward rather than back. Indeed, the *Metamorphoses*, often interpreted as insisting upon change as the only constant, also limits it: we see how the world has come to be the way it is, and explanation brings a sense of naturalness as well as inevitability. Generally, Ovid does not say whether he thinks things are more different or more the same as a result of metamorphosis; sometimes a small change helps to clarify a fundamental identity. But this is a matter of perspective (if you have changed from a person into a flower, you are likely to think of that as a pretty big deal, whatever others might say!). We might usefully compare the apparent contradiction between Augustus's claim that he fought to 'restore' the Republic which had been falling apart, and the result of his actions, which was a monarchic dynasty. As with so many aspects of Ovid's work, the final judgement is left up to the reader: does the *Metamorphoses* criticize Augustus for arbitrarily imposing his will on a helpless landscape? Does it celebrate the chain of events that has led to Rome's empire?

Indeed, had Augustus but realized it, the seemingly frivolous poetry of Ovid was perhaps the best advertisement of the stability he achieved during his regime. For by the turn of the millennium (not a date that would have existed in the Roman calendar), Rome had more or less settled down after a hundred years of slow-but-steady breakdown and increasing lawlessness, officially ended by Augustus's victory in the battle of Actium in 31 BCE, although it took some further years for all enemies to be eliminated. Precisely how and why this happened is well beyond the scope of this book. But it is clear that it was a tentative process, in which none of the actors, including Augustus himself, knew exactly how to proceed.

Scholars of this period emphasize that the changes that collectively took place to form the Augustan age were sometimes gradual, sometimes sudden, sometimes well-received and sometimes renegotiated. But they were above all comprehensive: there was almost no event, place or circumstance that pertained to a Roman of Ovid's time in which he could not see the hand of Augustus, or Caesar before him. A single, but important, one of these was Caesar's calendar reforms of 46 BCE, which imposed order on what had been chaos; Augustus instituted further modifications. It was not that the Romans did not have a calendar before, merely that it had not been revised for some time, and that the practice of inserting additional months, originally religious, had been used to political ends so many times (most notably, to delay elections) that one might be celebrating a harvest festival in springtime. Caesar and especially Augustus capitalized on the opportunity to control time, instituting and reviving religious and civic festivals, some in honour of family members. Indeed, the period just before the turn of the millennium was heralded as a literally new age, celebrated by the Saecular Games (17 BCE, memorialized for us by Horace's *Carmen Saeculare*). So the *Fasti*, Ovid's poem on the calendar, turns out to be especially timely, reflecting contemporary interest in how different structures of time interact with one another.

And there were many other manifestations of an organizing hand. Augustus slowly but by no means inevitably amassed a wide variety of traditional powers for himself. They all had Republican precedents, but their concentration in him, rather than distribution over many individuals, marked a break with the past. Beyond this, the emperor involved himself in nearly every aspect of life in the newly founded empire. One of the subjects on which he seems to have felt strongly was his belief that Rome had degenerated from its once-noble simplicity (this need not be literally true; a nostalgic view of the past is common to many politicians, and also reflects long-standing Roman tradition). In order to put Rome back on its proper footing, Augustus supported a series of moral reforms, among them legislation that restricted marriage between different classes, and made adultery a more serious, and also a more public, crime than it had been. Scholars have difficulty knowing what to make of these laws: they are literally unprecedented, in that such matters had not before been considered appropriate subjects for legislation. While the reforms of Augustus and his advisers of the grain supply, taxation, governmental bureaucracy and the rebuilding of decrepit public buildings are normally seen as easily explicable acts of rebuilding after a traumatic time, Augustus's focus on the family sticks out like a sore thumb. But it may also be that moderns are tempted to see this set of laws as more innovative than it actually was, because of our assumption that there is such a thing as a 'private life'. At any rate, it was possible for Augustus to claim – and even to believe – that the Roman gods were deeply concerned with every aspect of their people's lives, and his restructuring of the beliefs and laws about marriage and sex is not necessarily different from his reorganization of civic space.

The Augustan laws on marriage, specifically the *Lex Julia de maritandis ordinibus* and *Lex Julia de adulteriis coercendis* of 18 BCE, encompassed legislation on a variety of matters which had earlier been considered family concerns. They mandated marriage by a certain age and remarriage within certain time limits after divorce and widowhood; they limited the inheritances that could be given or received by the childless; they forbade the senatorial class from contracting legal marriages with freed persons; they made adultery a public crime, rather than, as had been customary, one handled within a household, and imposed severe penalties on it. This latter point is worth restating, as its significance is often underestimated: before these laws, the sexual practices of Roman citizens had been more or less a private matter, up to families to police. Some families, and some individuals, seem to have cared deeply about monogamy within marriage, and others did not. After the laws were passed, who slept with whom became subject to the courts, but ultimately to the moral beliefs of Augustus. These marriage laws reflect in microcosm what scholars see as a pervasive Augustan practice of mixing categories of public and private: in becoming the 'father of his fatherland' (*pater patriae*), Augustus perhaps naturally took on the regulatory functions that had traditionally been given to the male head of household (the *paterfamilias*). Moderns are likely to think of Augustus's acts as incursions into the domestic sphere, but the Augustan period was largely responsible for defining a sphere henceforth known as domestic.

The *Lex Poppia Poppaea* of 9 CE is generally agreed to have been a modification of the Julian laws, lightening penalties and extending time periods, and this may provide evidence for the unpopularity of the original legislation, as do a number of ancient sources; the Julian laws, in fact, are one of the single most common features of Augustus's reign mentioned by later authors. They seem to be a relatively rare instance of an Augustan misstep, and Ovid's poetry may reflect a genuine tension between (what it presents as) the freewheeling sexual morality of the time and how Augustus thought things ought to be.

So too, at least if the attention of later legal experts is any indication, these laws were notoriously difficult to interpret, as they seem to have attempted to divide women into just two mutually exclusive categories: those of the upper classes, whom one could marry, and those who were not respectable. The reality was surely a bit more complicated (take, for example, women working in shops, who might be legally married and even admired by their neighbours as moral exemplars, but, because of their class, were not protected by the Augustan laws against rape). But Ovid obligingly – and disingenuously – plays along with the Augustan dichotomy, stating at the beginning of the *Ars* that the work is *not* to be read by matrons, concluding 'there is no crime in my poem' (1.31–4, with an untranslatable pun on *crimen*, crime and *carmen*, poem). He reiterates the official distinction between women in near-identical form in *Ars* 2, three times in *Ars* 3, and in *Fas.* 4. and *Tr.* 2. Interestingly, the status of the elegiac *puella* is never really made clear, by Ovid or other poets: many assume that she is a member of the lower classes, perhaps a freedwoman prostitute, but elegists sometimes, distressingly, refer to her as having a *vir*, a word which could mean 'main patron' or something of the sort, but which is most naturally taken in Latin to denote a husband.

It is, of course, dangerous to draw any conclusions about either man's personal morality from their public stances; Suetonius's biography of Augustus portrays him as much more like his contemporaries than his public persona might suggest, claiming that his friends selected women and girls for him, stripping and inspecting them (*matronae* and *virgines*, Suet. *Aug.* 69.1; probably not true). There is also, notoriously, the difficulty Augustus had with his daughter and granddaughter, both named Julia and both relegated for adultery – the second in the very same year as Ovid was sent to Tomis. The emperor seems to have treated these instances as family matters rather than public ones – but here again we are faced with the fact that Augustus was extremely successful in making his personal life appear public, and simultaneously in making Rome part of his own extended family.

Patronage

Beyond new laws, another facet of life that was in flux was the notion of patronage. Elite Romans had long sponsored artistic works in their own honour (most regularly, but not exclusively, for military achievements), but this habit starts to take on a different look in the last century BCE, as the number of patrons dwindles to a handful. Eventually – indeed, even during Ovid's lifetime – all possible patrons are connected to the emperor by blood or long-standing intimacy, so Augustus's preferences in art and literature almost inevitably become more important than anyone else's. Among Augustus's advisers was the equestrian (knight) Maecenas, who is sometimes styled a 'minister of culture', and who became a patron of the arts, especially of poets such as Horace, Vergil and Propertius (all in the generation just before, but overlapping, with Ovid's own). Each of these three authors suggests – if we read them literally – that Maecenas has been clamouring for poetry to celebrate the rule of Augustus, and each in his own way does express at least a limited form of support for the new regime. There is lively debate about how seriously we are to take their statements of coercion, which simultaneously imply deep concern on the part of the emperor about what poets are up to (and so emphasize their importance) and document their refusal to give him what he wants (which suggests that it was something of a non-issue). It would be astonishing if Augustus's grand schemes did *not* include poetry to celebrate his achievements, given its importance to contemporary Romans, but we should not imagine that he simply wanted cheerleaders to mouth his praises. Vergil's *Aeneid* is the poem which has most frequently been examined to discover whether it is imperial panegyric or, alternately, subversive slander; recent work on the poem sees it as double in nature, reflecting both the sense that things had changed, probably for the better, and the wish that the change had not needed to be quite so violent.

In contrast to those poets in the immediately preceding generation, Ovid does not seem to have had a patron. In the *Epistulae Ex Ponto*, he mentions connections to the family of Messalla, a patron of Tibullus and some lesser-known poets, but there are no earlier poems dedicated to him, which suggests that he was not formally Ovid's patron. The *Epistulae Ex Ponto*, in fact, depict a stage in the development of patronage literature, as they show Ovid exhorting multiple possible patrons to assist him. Ovid's own tentative steps toward working out what would happen when Augustus died (he seems to have hoped for the support of the emperor's adopted grandson, Germanicus, and eschewed appealing to Tiberius) mirror the emperor's own much more robust efforts to stabilize things from beyond the grave. It is not until after Augustus's death and Tiberius's accession to the throne that it became apparent that it was possible for Augustus to transfer his unique personal authority, cobbled together over many years, to another person. But Ovid, for his part, seems to assume that Augustus will be able to choose his successor, and that the peace brought by Augustus was a permanent one.

This section has provided some context about the world in which Ovid lived. Despite what seems to many readers like an obvious, even inevitable, tension between Augustanism and Ovidianism, it has also emphasized that these battle-lines were not (yet) fully drawn. Finally, it has suggested in a number of ways that Ovid was a profoundly Roman poet. We shall return to Rome later, but, for now, let us remember that Ovid wrote (half of?) the *Fasti*, a poem on the Roman calendar and religious and civic history. So too, the *Ars* praises Rome for its cosmopolitan nature, which means that you can find everything you are looking for in it (1.55–6). He happens to be referring to women; his examples are 'dusky Indians' and 'a Greek girl'. This is, presumably, not Augustus's main concern, and the poet's immediately following 'erotic topography of Rome', where he points out places to pick up women which coincidentally (or perhaps not) bear the names of members of Augustus's family, is likely to have made matters even worse. But surely the general sentiment, that Rome contains everything of value, is in keeping with what Augustus himself would have believed.

Ovid, then, is similar to Augustus, as well as serving as his negative mirror reflection. Like many key historical figures, Augustus shaped the world in his own image, and the characteristics of Augustus become those of his age. The Augustan period, taken broadly, was one which saw consolidation of knowledge in a wide variety of fields. We see a concentration of manuals or comprehensive treatments of such diverse topics as history, mythology, geography and architecture appearing right around the turn of the millennium, and it is reasonable to see Ovid's *Metamorphoses* as a similar effort to categorize the world. The emperor's willingness to experiment also finds an analogue in Ovid's own generic and poetic efforts. Each, over a long career, works from within a traditional form and, through a series of small steps and bold leaps, changes the face of his chosen subject forever. Augustus created a new form of government, one which melded traditional Republican ways of doing things with the authority of a monarch; while his successors paid lip service to his accomplishments, for various reasons, some had a longer afterlife than others. Ovid created several new forms of literature, breathing new life into elegiac poetry by a series of extraordinary manoeuvres, some of which found immediate imitators and others of which were less successful. And the two men, both products of their age, each attempted to create a delicate equilibrium: Augustus was, after all, officially only 'first among equals'; Ovid for his part needed both to be understood and to be misunderstood.

Repetition-Compulsion and Ovidian Excess

2.1 Now You See Him, Now You Still See Him: Ovidian Narrative Style and Metre

Metre

We return to the poetry of Ovid. Because we have seen evidence for his versatility of material and approach, it may come as a surprise to find that Ovid's formal poetic decisions were fairly uniform. All of his work, with the exception of the *Metamorphoses* and the tragic *Medea*, was written in the elegiac metre, and beyond this, there is a recognizable 'shape' to his poetry; an Ovidian line is often instantly recognizable (except when he is parodying an earlier poet – and sometimes even then Ovid shines through!).

Ancient Greek and Latin poetry is figured language not because of rhyme-scheme, as is much modern poetry, but by metre, or a patterned series of long and short syllables. Elegiac poetry is written in a metre nearly identical to dactylic hexameter, which is the metre of epic poetry (i.e. the poetry of Homer and Vergil, among others, about 'heroic deeds'). The dactylic (named for the Greek 'finger', because each metrical foot, like each finger, has one longer and two shorter units) hexameter (because there are six of them; hex = six in Greek) was used for the Homeric poems, and adapted to Latin by early Roman poets. Vergil is generally agreed to have perfected the Latin hexameter, fitting intractable Latin words into the originally Greek metre; Ovid did the same for the elegiac couplet, and his verses are generally even more fluid than Vergil's.

The elegiac couplet, also a Greek metre in origin, developed in Latin in two directions: first, short epigrams (poems of four or six lines long), sometimes funerary, sometimes with a witty point at the end, and second, into a kind of poetry called 'elegy', practiced by Catullus, Gallus, Tibullus, Propertius and Ovid (the middle three, so far as we know, wrote exclusively elegiacs). The couplet may have etymological origins in lament, and it retains associations with sadness for the Romans, and even into the modern period. Formally, the elegiac couplet has two parts: the first line is a dactylic hexameter (six feet of dactyls, usually written – ˘˘ |), and the second, often called the 'distich', takes the first two-and-a-half feet of the hexameter and doubles them (– ˘˘ – ˘˘ – ‖ – ˘˘ – ˘˘ –). Any two of the short syllables can be replaced by a long one (though this almost never happens in the next-to-last foot of the hexameter, and the metre of the second half of the distich is invariable). The metre is really a variant of the hexameter, one which provides a natural break every two lines, and Ovid (and most who come after him, in any language) uses those as sense-breaks as well. The metrical similarities between elegy and epic mean that direct quotation is possible, and Ovid often takes advantage of this, usually 'splicing in' epic to provide an incongruous model or to deflate the context in which the line or phrase originally appeared.

Because of the close similarities between the epic and elegiac metres, Ovid regularly draws attention to the fact of his almost-but-not-quite status as an epic poet, and 'worries' about whether his unstable and top-heavy couplets (because they have an odd number of feet, eleven (6 in one line + 2.5 + 2.5 in the other) in place of the epic twelve, evenly distributed over two lines) can bear the 'weight' of his subject matter when it ventures toward the serious; this conceit appears most frequently in places like the *Fasti* or the exilic poetry, where Ovid uses it to draw attention to his expansion of the traditional boundaries of elegy. So, for instance, the *Fasti* says it will focus on the family of Augustus, rather than the ruler's military deeds: the latter is far too 'heavy' for the metre. But Ovid also puns on the similar vocabulary of metrical and corporeal feet, as when the goddess Elegy herself appears in *Am.* 3.1, limping as if one foot is longer than the other, or when the personified book of poetry emphasizes the 'trembling' of its alternate feet (*Tr.* 3.1.56). The best example of a foot-pun, however, is Ovid's first: at *Am.* 1.1.1–4, the poet says he was in the midst of writing epic poetry, but Cupid came along, laughing, and 'stole a foot' from his verse; he is therefore forced to write elegiac poetry. Ovid also claims that everything he wrote came out, involuntarily, in couplets (quoted in Section 1.1); the statement should be taken with a pinch of salt, and exemplifies Ovid's typically dismissive attitude toward the labours of poetic composition which so many of his contemporaries emphasize. It also shows that he recognized his own mastery of the form.

Ancient metre is not, or not quite, the same as genre, but metres did have particular kinds of subject-matter associated with them. Hexameter is grand and stately, the metre of other kinds of serious poetry as well as of epic. (Lucretius's scientific explication of the world and Horace's philosophical letters are each written in hexameters, and so is satire, a kind of poetry which expresses outrage at the evils of the world.) Elegiac poetry, at least before Ovid got to it, was more limited in scope: starting from its origins (in Latin) with Catullus, who seems to have narrowed the broader Greek conception of the metre, it was poetry about love, usually unfortunate and with little chance of happy resolution.

Elegy before Ovid seems to focus on a single amatory relationship (or at least, on one at a time). Its key figures are the lover, who is also the poet, and the object of his love, usually but not exclusively female, and called the *puella*. The poet provides us with a one-sided view of his relationship, such that it is tempting to agree with him that the *puella* is greedy, manipulative, faithless and evil, even if she is also irresistible. But the persona of the lover is ironic, and we may be meant to see through it to a more complicated truth underneath: he is not always to be trusted when he describes his relationship. And indeed, as we shall see, most of Ovid's narrators are unreliable in one respect or another.

Ovid's development and expansion of previous love elegy demonstrates his capacity for innovation within an established genre.

His *puella*, Corinna, is barely fleshed-out, such that many readers have trouble believing that she has any 'real' analogue. This was true for Propertius's *puella* Cynthia as well, in the sense that we never got much physical description, but Cynthia has a distinct, and frightening, personality of the sort that Corinna never does. Rather, the figure of Corinna is a kind of puppet or doll, placed by the poet into a variety of situations so that he can react to them: Corinna dyes her hair; Corinna takes up with a rich soldier; Corinna invites herself into the lover's bedroom and then plays hard-to-get. The process he follows is not wholly different from that of Tibullus or Propertius, but Ovid has a way of laying bare the conceits as he employs them, a tactic which encourages critical distance, or playful detachment. This is, in fact, not so dissimilar from his habit of undermining serious moments, discussed later in this section. It is noteworthy too that, for Ovid, love poetry comes before the love object; Corinna is not introduced until the fifth poem of the *Amores*, after the poet has been forced by Cupid's 'theft' of one of his metrical 'feet' to write love poetry instead of epic, and after he has already pronounced himself in love.

Ovidian Style

There are many distinct features of Ovid's style, and the best way of summarizing them is to say that their combined effect draws the reader effortlessly through the Latin; we might call it a 'straightforward' style, which – at least apparently – contains few fancy tricks. But this is not quite true, as we have already seen the ways in which Ovid's surface simplicity hides complexity, as when he uses puns (he notes himself that the best art 'hides through its own art' *Met.* 10.252). His style has been called both 'cinematic' (because of the sometimes-awkward 'cuts' between scenes, and the panoramic vistas he depicts) and 'painterly' (because of his attention to small but telling detail). His metrical patterns are fairly regular, however dexterous, and tend to use more short syllables than long, which means both that Ovid can get more words in a line than other poets, and that one seems to reach the end of the line more quickly. His vocabulary is not difficult, despite the frequent choice of an unexpected word, which may give pause. This ease of passage through the text is an especially welcome feature to those newer to the language – and the pleasure of reading Ovid is well worth the toil of learning Latin – but it also has a disquieting element: we regularly find ourselves lost, not quite certain how we have got from familiar ground to somewhere subtly different; often this disequilibrium is reflected in abrupt alterations of tone.

Ovid's genius lies in incongruous combination rather than in outright invention, and, indeed, Latin poetry as a whole is much more interested in varying a series of established themes than in creating new ones. So, for instance, elegy as a genre had always been voracious, attempting to incorporate everything in its path. This is true within the poems – note for instance the regular metaphors utilized to describe the elegiac relationship, of which much the most developed are the notions of love as slavery, love as war, and love as a kind of hunt; Ovid explicitly works out the implications of these metaphors, especially in *Ars* 1 and 2. It is even truer metapoetically, as we see from the elegists' regular declarations that they would have been happy to write a more dignified sort of poetry, except that their girlfriends won't allow it: in addition to Cupid's intervention at *Am.* 1.1.1–4, *Am.* 2.1.11–20 has Ovid writing a big epic battle scene, when his girlfriend 'slams the door'; immediately, he drops epic and returns to elegy, his 'proper weapon' – and see too *Am.* 2.18.11–18, where tragedy gets a similar treatment. This refusal (formally, a *recusatio*) is consistently undermined, as the elegists, and especially Ovid, manage to sneak in through the back door everything they have ostentatiously banned from the front. No epic allowed! But epic lovemaking in the *Amores*, and characters from epic, especially in moments in their traditional stories where they behave un-epically; eventually, at least for Ovid, there is also a massive epic(-like) poem.

There is much more to say about the qualities of the *Metamorphoses*; as a start I offer a few examples of Ovidian subversion of epic language and themes. We start with the deeply moving death scene of Pyramus in

Fig. 3 Mosaic of Pyramus and Thisbe.

Metamorphoses 4 (useful to Shakespeare in a number of places). Believing his beloved Thisbe to be dead, Pyramus stabs himself to death. 'As he lay on the earth, gore spurted far and wide, not differently from when a pipe is burst where the lead is weak and it sends out much water through the small aperture with a hissing sound, cleaving the air with its blows'.

This technical but wildly creative description of a broken pipe becomes grotesque when one remembers that it is being used to depict the blood spurting out of a slashed body. The Latin suggests, better than my translation can, a cartoonish nature to this scene of violence, which perhaps makes it less disturbing – and indeed, Ovid often handles violence with such distancing gestures. But the image of Tereus, who cuts out the tongue of his sister-in-law Philomela (he has just raped her, and is worried that she will tattle), is harder to explain away: 'the utmost tip of the tongue quivers, it lies on the dark earth, trembling and murmuring, and, as the tail of a mutilated snake is accustomed to leap about, it twitches and, dying, it seeks the feet of its owner' (*Met.* 6.557–60). Many readers feel that there is something faintly immoral about maintaining an amused distance from such intimate violence: we smile, but are discomfited. In a slightly different way, it has been argued that the *Ibis*, a poem composed of hundreds of curses against Ovid's unnamed enemy, regains humour precisely because of its lack of restraint: readers are first taken aback, then appalled and, finally, amused by his vitriol. Quintilian, a later writer, did not approve of Ovid's style, calling him 'too much a lover of his own cleverness' (*Institutio Oratoria* 10.1.88) – and many generations shared this opinion.

Ovid's love of the incongruous meshes well with the importance of rhetoric in ancient education; the upper classes – the only ones who received formal education – trained their children to speak well in public, and above all else, in forensic and political contexts. Boys (rarely girls) memorized great literature, and then spent years working out ever more complicated speeches on a series of set topics. We could assume that Ovid had received this education, but, as it happens, Seneca the Elder tells us he did, focusing in on the stylistic features we too notice in Ovid (*Controversiae* 2.2.8–12): he describes Ovid as 'not ignorant of his flaws, but fond of them', and tells an instructive story whereby friends of Ovid asked permission to remove from his poetry three verses (presumably those they found most tasteless); Ovid agreed, provided he could keep three verses immune. Perhaps unsurprisingly, the lists were the same: it is clear that Ovid knew what he was doing.

A number of Ovidian passages have their roots in school exercises such as how to make a difficult choice, usually in the persona of a historical or mythological character. There is an especially good example of the 'tragic soliloquy' at *Met.* 8.460–514 (complete with wordplay), where Althaea struggles with the question of whether she should avenge the death of her brothers by killing her son (who has killed them); she can do so easily, for his life at birth was linked to a log that had been in the fire: she need only toss the log back on to the fire and watch it burn. Ovid often, but not always, puts such internal conflicts into direct speech; they are recognizably elements of the Greek and Roman tragic stage, and Ovid is likely to be drawing on lost models for many of these figures (most often, at least in Ovid, women). So too, Ovid's poetry regularly features another Roman homework topic: characters arguing one or the other side of a case, or both (this is most clearly represented in *Met.* 13, in the paired speeches of Odysseus and Ajax about which of them should be awarded the arms of the dead Achilles). In addition to large-scale speeches and internal monologues, however, Ovid's works abound with the rhetorical turn of phrase, the wordplay which amuses but perhaps also carries a deeper meaning, and even the pun. Every reader will have a favourite moment, although Ovid's work is studded with gems so liberally that it may be hard to choose just one.

Perhaps one of the more poignant kinds of Ovidian juxtapositions comes in the tale of Narcissus – one of Ovid's most popular stories – where the beautiful young hero, constantly pursued by amorous youths and women but spurning them, is finally punished for his selfishness. So beautiful is Narcissus that he has only to catch sight of himself in a still pool to fall in love. Puzzled at first, he eventually realizes what is going on, and exclaims, 'what I desire is with me – and my abundance creates a lack! Would that I were able to leave from my own body! Here is a new prayer for a lover: I wish that what I love were further away!' (3.466–9; the Latin contains a pun on *copia*, abundance, and *inopia*, lack). As often, Ovid's words capture a larger truth: sometimes desire feels as if it would be satisfied only by literally sharing one consciousness, or one body, with a loved one. And the *Metamorphoses* are full of such tensions between absence and presence. Myrrha, in Book 10, tortured by an incestuous desire for her father, laments that their current close relationship precludes an even closer one. The hunter Actaeon is summoned by his companions to watch the dogs bringing down a handsome stag. Unfortunately for him, he *is* the stag, having been turned into one by an angry goddess: Ovid notes, 'he would, indeed, have wished to be away, but he was present' (*Met.* 3.247; for more on Actaeon, see Section 3.2). The plights of both Actaeon and Narcissus are poignant in the abstract; given each man's situation, they are also just plain funny. This combination of the serious with the laughable is one of the most striking stylistic features of Ovid's poetry. Sometimes the

Fig. 4 Narcissus.

incongruity is profound, as with Narcissus; sometimes it is 'merely' verbal, as in *Met.* 2 when the god Hermes takes literally a mortal's insistence that she 'will not move from this spot' and turns her into a rock.

Sometimes Ovidian inconsistency comes simply from exploring a trope beyond where it had usually been taken, as when the poet wholeheartedly embraces the Julian claim of descent from Venus and calls Augustus a 'cousin' of her son Cupid (*Am.* 1.2.51), or when he just as enthusiastically takes seriously earlier poets' discussions of Augustus's quasi-divinity, and compares Jupiter's Olympus to Augustus's Palatine in *Met.* 1. Great Romans had regularly, following great Greeks, cast themselves as descendants or even incarnations of the Olympian gods, but they do not seem to have expected others to work out the full implications of these analogies. The question of how, when and where, Augustus began to be thought of as a god is well beyond our scope; Ovid's breezy assimilation of head man to head god may reflect the kind of thing people were actually thinking and saying, or may instead have been perceived as deeply blasphemous, *even* if it was the kind of thing people were saying. However we are to understand it, no other contemporary literature comes quite so close to deifying the living emperor.

Ovid's habit of keeping the reader off-balance is perhaps most evident in the *Metamorphoses*, but it is also present in the *Fasti*. And the two poems have many other similarities: as we have noted, they seem to have been composed more or less at the same time, one in elegiacs and the other in dactylic hexameters. They tell some of the same stories; the one that has received the most scholarly attention is the kidnapping of Persephone by her uncle, in *Met.* 5 and *Fas.* 4. But even when they tell different stories, they use many of the same themes (we have already noticed the ways in which the *Metamorphoses* treats its characters as if they have Roman values, or as if they are characters in an elegy; the *Fasti* does much the same). The two works are Ovid's largest-scale poems, each providing a continuous narrative. As such they offer the opportunity to examine a further series of important themes. Each of the poems suggests that it tells a complete story. But one of Ovid's points is that no story is ever complete, both in the sense that it is impossible to provide every detail, and that *these* stories, about the history of everything and about the history of the Romans respectively, are for Ovid and his audience ongoing events, liable to further revision (a point already made by Vergil, on whom see Section 2.2). The point is worth expanding: one of Ovid's main strategies in these poems is to juxtapose stories with no apparent connection (see Section 3.3, for an awkward transition in the *Fasti* which has political import). Another is to invent a connection that turns out to be specious; for instance, many of the mythological exempla in the *Amores* and *Ars Amatoria* either have only a superficial connection to the main event, or open up into disturbing implications which seem unintended: the (male) lover in *Ars* 1 is told that he needn't work so hard, because women are naturally amorous, but the examples adduced (including Pasiphae, who falls in love with a bull and jealously sacrifices her attractive cow-rivals) are hardly encouraging.

The epic *Metamorphoses* begins with a cosmogony, then re-founds the world not once but twice: first there is a flood which destroys everyone but the pious Deucalion and Pyrrha, then a fire arising from Phaethon's ill-fated journey in the chariot of the sun, which leaves much of the earth uninhabitable. The *Fasti* also has two cosmogonies: it begins with Janus, who claims to be an avatar of Chaos himself, and then re-begins in Book 5, when a muse retells, with variations, the separation of the elements. Both poems also feature gods as primary characters. But each poem is nonetheless resolutely human-centred: this is so not merely because the gods behave like large versions of human beings (a technique as old as Homer); it is also that human action, choice and will are featured prominently.

Narrators

Some kinds of story function by drawing the reader in, and by seamlessly allowing her to imagine herself part of the scene. The Ovidian narrator, by contrast, is fairly intrusive, often in banal ways, and prevents readers from forgetting that they are only metaphorically present. So, for instance, he will interrupt a story to tell us something obvious: in *Met.* 5, one of the Muses, setting the scene for a tale she is telling to Minerva, explains that the king Pyreneus invited them into his home 'to avoid the threatening sky and the rain – for it was raining'. This unnecessary detail has the effect of distancing readers from the story being told, at least until Ovid's compelling style draws us in again. And sometimes the intrusion is salacious rather than gratuitous, as when Ovid, annoyed by the sunrise, elucidates the goddess Dawn's eagerness to leave her bed: her partner Tithonus is old and decrepit (*Am.* 1.13; she had obtained eternal life for him, but not eternal youth, so he eventually shrivelled into a cricket).

Beyond this, narrators in Ovid (whether the poetic persona or a character in a poem) also regularly offer commentary which is out of place or even downright manipulative. So, for instance, *Am.* 1.7 begins with a scene of repentance: Ovid has struck his *puella* and, in an agony of regret, berates himself via a series of mythological examples, the import of which is that the *puella* is beautiful when she weeps.

He ends by urging her to hit him back: 'do not spare my eyes nor my hair – anger aids even the weakest hands'. But then, in an abrupt shift, the poem continues 'or at least, so that the unfortunate evidence of my crime is no longer present, put your re-done hair back in order'. The final couplet, suggesting that the matter can be fixed with a quick combing, undermines all that has gone before. The reader is left with two choices about the event: either we trust the lover, and see that he was merely humouring the overly dramatic *puella*, or we consider him a remorseless cad, who, having beaten his girlfriend, wants to minimize the consequences.

Two poems in particular feature problematic narrators, the *Ars* and the *Fasti*. In the first, Ovid's didactic poem about how to find love and keep it, the speaker assures us that he does not, as so many poets do, rely on divine inspiration. Rather, he is a poet of 'experience' (*usus, Ars* 1.29), so his tried-and-tested system is (almost) guaranteed. So far so good. But we soon discover that the teacher's qualifications are suspect. Perhaps we can dismiss with a chuckle his claim that poets make the best lovers (*Ars* 3.534, addressed to women!). But it is certainly distressing to find him giving advice which he cannot himself follow: at *Ars* 2.167–74, he urges lovers to avoid striking the *puella*, mostly because she will pretend that you've broken something, and then you will have to pay for a new one. The passage continues by explaining that he himself cannot always do as he suggests, and that once he did mess up her hair (the situation detailed at great length in *Am.* 1.7, if we accept his version of the story) and had to buy her new clothes. So too, he urges us to put up with a rival (*Ars* 2.547–50), but says that he cannot; he claims at *Ars* 2.639–40 to tell of previous love affairs 'sparingly', a statement undermined by three books of *Amores*. Finally, in the middle of the *Remedia Amoris*, he tells us that he himself was unable to cure his love for a particular *puella* (311–14). How can we, with so much less experience, be expected to do better than the man who teaches us?

The narrator of the *Fasti* is in even worse shape. But at least he does not claim to have all the answers: in fact, what he has are a series of questions, which he puts to one after another of the divine or human figures who appear to him, a device taken from Callimachus's *Aetia*, in which that poet had held a series of discussions with the Muses about the causes of various events. Let us leave aside the deliberate silliness of some of his questions (surely Ovid could figure out by himself that small gifts of cash are given at the new year to encourage prosperity, *Fas.* 1.188). It is much more peculiar that Ovid's divine interlocutors do not know the answers, or rather, that they offer several competing options, and the poet offers us no help. For instance, the namesake for the month of June is never really resolved; three goddesses, *Juno*, her daughter Hebe ('youth', ju*ventas* in Latin), and Concord (who says the month comes from the *join*ing of two peoples to make Rome) engage in an ugly wrangle. Ovid (perhaps having learned from Paris's experience in judging the divine beauty contest which started the Trojan War) wisely refuses to arbitrate, but in the process, fails in his self-appointed duty: again, the author behind the narrator shows his hand.

Beyond the narrators themselves, narrative transitions, especially in the *Metamorphoses*, are also instructive. Metamorphosis itself is usually a closural device, since it either focuses on the dissolution of a human being or on the origin of some new artefact (plant, bird, rock formation). In Ovid's *perpetuum . . . carmen* ('never-ending poem', *Met.* 1.4), however, it becomes merely another tool in the toolbox. For example, as we noted earlier with Phaethon's sisters (see Section 1.1), sometimes metamorphosis is tacked on at the end of a story, without much connection. But sometimes metamorphosis is not quite the end, as occurs when Callisto is turned by Juno into a bear as punishment for suffering rape from Jupiter, and later turned into a constellation (see Section 3.1). So too, the philosopher Pythagoras delivers the longest speech of the poem in *Met.* 15, claiming that everything is in flux. Each individual change, the poem suggests, is relatively permanent, but the emphasis on perpetual change suggests that there are many more stories which could be told, or at least that we are only hearing selected portions of the stories we do hear. The transitions in the *Fasti*, and its awkward juxtapositions of 'unrelated' material, are equally interesting, but are only beginning to receive scholarly attention (see Section 3.3 for one especially problematic example). In some ways, this is inherent to the nature of that poem: what happens on 7 January may not, in fact, have a lot in common with what happens on 6 January. But such a claim underestimates the role of the narrator, who doesn't tell everything he knows, and doesn't know everything he tries to tell.

Our focus on narrative technique has helped to clarify a key aspect of Ovidian style, namely, his interest in how a story is told. This could be illustrated from anywhere in the corpus, but let us focus on the *Heroides*, the series of letters from (mostly) fictional characters. The single *Heroides* broaden the genre of elegy in a number of ways. They tell a story we already know, not only because elegy tends to be fairly repetitive and features stereotypical situations, but in the sense that we know this *precise* story, normally from a heavy hitter among Ovid's poetic predecessors (more on Ovidian repetitiveness in Section 2.2). For these are not merely letters written by women to the men who abandon them, but letters written by, say, Medea, shortly before she decides to kill her children, or by Dido as she is coming to the realization that Aeneas is going to leave her. As such, they allow Ovid to focus in on the kinds of issues that interest him everywhere, especially the point that *how* a story goes is very much dependent upon who tells it to you. We have already seen several ways he does this in the *Amores* and *Metamorphoses*. Tapping into a vein of story material that already exists allows Ovid to explore the ironies caused by different viewpoints. The heroines used to be objects of pity, as scholars believed that we, having read the 'canonical' versions of their texts, knew more than they did. More recently, it has been suggested that the heroines' letters radically undermine the very notion of a 'canonical' version. We 'know' that Briseis, Achilles' war prize in Homer's *Iliad*, is of importance to the story only symbolically, because she stands for the status that Achilles gained when she was awarded to him, and that he lost when Agamemnon took her away. But perhaps that is only Achilles' version of the story, as he sulks in his tent, or only the version Homer was interested in; Briseis's own rendition, told in *Heroides* 3, might well seem more compelling, or truer, especially where it weaves itself into the story we already 'know'.

So, for instance, when she describes her departure from Achilles, she notes that the two heralds, Eurybates and Talthybius, 'each, casting his eyes at the other, wondered silently where our love was' (*Her.* 3.11–12). In the *Iliad*, these are the very heralds who come to remove Briseis, but they are (presumably) looking at one another primarily in fear lest Achilles resort to his characteristic violence; it is not clear that they even know who Briseis is, let alone that she and Achilles are in love. So Briseis is perhaps simply mistaken (or perhaps she tells a different version of the truth). But she seems closer to the mark when she accuses Achilles of laziness, even cowardice: 'battle is dangerous; playing the lyre and singing and love are pleasant' (*Her.* 3.116). Ovid suggests, as often, that there is more to the story than we usually learn: even if we do not choose to privilege Briseis's story over Homer's, reading it is likely to change the way we read portions of the *Iliad*. In some ways, this is a strikingly modern gesture, similar to recent interventions into and interactions with classic literature.

It is also a gesture that can be read as appropriative, or even hostile. For it may be the case that Ovid gives his heroines only enough rope to hang themselves with: they *think* they are agents, trying to bring about a desired outcome, but we, with the force of centuries of reading habits, force them back into their straitjackets – so, for instance, Dido may simply make a mistake, or show her own lack of charity, when she blames Aeneas for losing his wife Creusa in the sack of Troy (*Her.* 7.71–86). But Dido also draws attention to an attitude toward this portion of the *Aeneid* that many modern readers share: how hard would it have been, really, for Aeneas to put his father on his shoulders, take hold of his son in one hand and the *penates* in another, *and tell Creusa to keep hold of his cloak*? Of course, Vergil needs Aeneas to be unmarried by the time he gets to Latium – but Ovid's Dido still points up an awkward part of Vergil's story. It is difficult to discern Ovid's attitude toward the women of mythology whose stories he tells in the *Heroides*; many Ovidian narrators have an easy habit of misogyny, among other unpalatable characteristics, and it is easy to dismiss many of the heroines as ancillary to the 'real' stories of mythology. At the same time, the poet himself has given us such compelling portraits of the heroines that they often seem more genuine than, say, the lover of the *Amores*, who may amuse, but rarely evokes an emotional response. As so often, the reader of Ovid is ultimately unable to find a stable place from which to render judgement.

Fact and Fiction, Presence and Absence

Ovid also plays more directly with the 'reality effect' of personal poetry; it had been a standard ploy for poets to draw attention to the dividing line between fact and fiction, in part to highlight their own creative abilities, in part to serve as a screen for the 'naughtiness' (*nequitia*) of their personae. But Ovid goes much further both in making autobiographical statements and in undermining them. *Am.* 2.17, in the course of celebrating the poet's fame, observes, 'I know a girl who puts it about that she is Corinna – in order to be so, what *wouldn't* she be willing to give?' With this sentence, the poet confirms our suspicions that his *puella* is a fiction (presumably at least some of his original readers would have known Corinna's identity, if she existed), and simultaneously teases us into believing that she might be – or become – a real person, *and* undermines his regular-but-implausible claims to faithfulness, by opening up the possibility of taking advantage of a groupie. 'She', whoever she is, is just an ordinary female reader of elegiac poetry, star-struck by the 'fame' Ovid seems to offer. In fact, she is quite a lot like the kind of woman Ovid addresses in *Ars* 3, who needs all the help she can get to be desirable. Later, as if the statement in 2.17 were not confusing enough, *Am.* 3.12 *does* lay claim to a corporeal Corinna, undermining, perhaps rendering null and void, the earlier poem: here the poet complains that it was his own words that made Corinna desirable to others: 'my girl has become an item for sale, thanks to my fault; she is pleasing because of my pimping; a lover has been brought to her with me as leader' (10–11).

As is often the case with Ovid, what looked to be merely about poetry turns out to have larger implications. We are warned by Ovid not to make the mistake of conflating a poetic narrative with the real world; but of course, he tells us this in his poetry (and thereby alludes to a long literary tradition of poets warning about just this mistake). Later in life, the exile poetry, especially *Tr.* 2, shows the dark side of this kind of identity play: you can get in serious trouble if someone with a different sensibility, and not a lot of patience, starts to wonder what is fiction and what fact. An obvious move would be for Ovid to try to clear up the misunderstanding by offering a clearer self-portrait. But strangely, or perhaps not so strangely after all, the remainder of his poetry reacts by doing *exactly the same thing*, by creating a story out of its own attempts to be understood properly, and by giving a variety of fairly unambiguous but mutually exclusive interpretations about the tale of Ovid-and-Augustus which refract and vary those of Ovid and his girl. Then again, once we have learned not to take Ovid at his own word, it is hard to know what statement he could make that would be assured of being taken at face value.

We have already noticed Ovid's interest in the twinned situations of presence and absence. Another way in which this is manifested is in his lifelong interest in letters, which he figures as 'speaking to you absent' (*Tr.* 3.3.17). What can a letter do in the world? What power do words (written or spoken) have? The letter, and indeed, writing as a whole, allows Ovid to engage both explicitly and implicitly with questions of the effectiveness of communication. Sometimes one side of the equation is focused on, sometimes the other. The exile poetry forces, or at least allows, Ovid to communicate with his readership in a rather different way than he previously had. As often in Ovid's own narratives, the exile poetry details an artist suffering for his art (see Section 3.2). Sometimes he is given the comfort of knowing that he has a kind of (poetic) immortality, and sometimes there is only suffering.

It is a concern of authors everywhere that they be understood rather than misunderstood, and there is always the possibility of misreading. Some authors ignore such anxieties; Ovid's response is to draw attention to the disjunction between intent and outcome, to depict failures of communication, ironic undertones and peculiar coincidences. Theorists regularly note the gap in Ovid between signifier and signified, i.e. that things do not quite mean what they seem to, or they draw attention to moments where interpretation does not work. To take one example: one of the storytellers in *Met.* 4 is Leuconoe, one of three sisters who refuses to participate in worship of Dionysus, preferring instead to stay inside and weave. She tells a story about a woman named Leucothoe, who was loved by the sun and eventually punished by her father with burial (she turns into frankincense). There is much to be said about this inset tale, but I draw attention only to the similarity of names between narrator and narratee: is it random coincidence? Does Leuconoe remember the story of Leucothoe because her name is familiar? Is that 'really' either woman's name? As readers, what are *we* to make of the story-within-a-story? – is there some larger point, some greater similarity we ought to be seeing between the stories? Where most authors would, if they wanted to tell both stories, separate them out so as to make things less confusing, or perhaps even change one of the names, Ovid seems to revel in teasing us with the overt interchangeability of his tales.

This is only one of dozens of places where Ovid forces readers to think carefully about stories-as-stories. We have already seen that he creates a plausible enough narrator in *Amores* 2.7 who hotly denies any hanky-panky with Corinna's slave Cypassis, only to have him blow the game in 2.8. Readers' reactions to being tricked will of course vary (some might simply abandon the work in disgust), but it seems likely that the reaction Ovid is seeking is amusement: we laugh at ourselves for believing him, and pity foolish Corinna, who is still in the position we used to be, before reading 2.8. In quite a number of time periods, this quintessentially Ovidian technique has made him unpopular; it runs directly counter to the Romantic notion that a poet should be sincere, honestly expressing his passions to us. In others, it is seen as one of his chief delights.

Another way in which Ovid plays with audience expectation is when his characters draw attention to their own status as characters in a poem, or reflect metapoetically upon the genre in which they find themselves – or even draw attention to ambiguities of their status. So, for instance, Achelous is both a (man-shaped, more or less) river-god and the river itself. In *Met.* 8, he (as god) invites a group of travellers into his home, because he (as river) is in flood and will otherwise sweep them away. In a slightly different vein, *Tr.* 1.2 tells the story of the epic-style storm which blasts Ovid out of the world of elegy into the dangerous world of adventure-epic: from here on out, elegy will become a rather different entity, and Ovid will regularly play the role of the Homeric hero Odysseus, suffering as he tries to return home (explicitly in *Tr.* 1.5, 3.11 and *EP* 4.10, but implicit throughout).

Ovid's habit of placing himself on the margin of his texts, commenting upon them as he writes them, undermining what has been said, is one of his most noticeable characteristics, and one which appealed also to some of his many imitators. His pose as a literary outsider, indeed, lasts throughout his entire poetic output. We have noticed other features of Ovid's poetry too, including a surface slickness, distracting rhetorical devices, pervasive irony, intrusive and unstable narration; these will recur throughout our discussion, as they contribute to understanding Ovidian poetics as a whole. Discussion has been reserved for the following section for what is perhaps the most prevalent of his characteristics, his habits of repetition and recycling.

2.2 Same Story, Different Day: Repetition and Reception

We have already noted that Latin poetry as a whole concentrated more on 'creative imitation', the combination of common themes in original ways, than on breaking new ground. But the best of the Latin poets succeeded in doing both, amalgamating previously incongruous elements to forge wholly individual works of art. Ovid is no exception; he seems to have displayed no 'anxiety of influence' about his predecessors, stealing like mad from the most important of his poetic forebears, and also, interestingly, from himself. This section concentrates on what is perhaps the most Ovidian of all Ovid's 'poetics of excess', his recycling, revision and repetition. Indeed, Ovid himself comments approvingly on the ability to return to the same font of inspiration, when he describes Odysseus as fascinating Calypso by his custom of 'telling the same story often in different ways' (*Ars* 2.128). In this context, which is one of seduction, it is high praise indeed to possess a trait that appeals to women so powerfully. Another mascot of Ovidian repetitiveness is the figure of Janus, the very first god to appear in the *Fasti*. He is the namesake of January, and he has two faces, so that he may look backward and forward at the same time. He stands for the repetitiveness of the calendar itself, which eventually gets around to the same place (or would, if Ovid had finished out the poem, and the year). Finally, he is in charge of opening (and closing) the gates of war, so he has an Augustan function too.

This section discusses first Ovid's use of his predecessors, then his regular, perhaps even compulsive, return to already complete poems, and finally, his more localized habit of repeating stories, themes and even of quoting from himself. It has long been noted that much of Ovid's poetry could not exist without his predecessors. This is true in more than the superficial way in which all artists are influenced by those who come before, for Ovid often responds directly and specifically to one particular poet. His *Amores* can be viewed as an extended rejoinder to the elegies of Propertius and, to a somewhat lesser extent, Tibullus. The *Heroides*, single and double, encompass bold retellings of some of the most well-known tales of nearly all of his important poetic predecessors – including Homer, Vergil, Euripides and Callimachus – in ways that can leave the reader breathless at his audacity. While tragedy by definition treats well-worn themes, the choice of Medea for his tragedy put him in direct competition with the greatest of the greats: in addition to the Euripidean version, there was Apollonius's treatment of her story in his Hellenistic epic, and we know of tragedies by Sophocles (seemingly, as many as four), Euripides (at least two others), and the Latin tragedians Ennius, Naevius, and Accius, which told different parts of Medea's story (see Section 3.1 for more on Medea). The *Ars* is more than a parody of Hesiod or Lucretius or even Vergil, but reading it in conjunction with those works helps to illuminate much that might have otherwise seemed puzzling about Ovid's appropriation of his predecessors' style and language. Later in his career, Ovidian recycling becomes even more intricate: the *Fasti* are rather like Callimachus's *Aetia*, as are the *Metamorphoses* – and each blends many dozens of other stories, narrative patterns, and even specific quotations into dazzling new combinations. The *Ibis* takes its name and subject matter from a similar work of Callimachus; the *Tristia* return to elegy's 'sad' roots and reconfigure Ovid as a mythical character, tossed about the seas like Odysseus seeking his Penelope, or left with only one friend, like Orestes with Pylades. The *Epistulae Ex Ponto* are in some ways the most original of Ovid's works (they bear many resemblances to Cicero's letters from exile, but there is no scholarly consensus about whether these are deliberate imitations or generic conventions).

Recycling

Ovid's use of other people's poetry is a complex topic, and one that has already filled many a book. I concentrate here only on Vergil, although Ovid's practice is similar with most of his literary forebears. In general, Ovid's habit is not simply to reuse a phrase or scene or motif, but to adapt it, to put it into a wholly new context which sheds unexpected light on the original, as we saw with his treatment of the women of the *Heroides* in Section 2.1. One large-scale way in which he accomplishes this is by the targeted expansion and contraction of narrative, especially when he treats canonical stories. So, for instance, Books 13 and 14 of Ovid's *Metamorphoses* cover some of the same events as Vergil's *Aeneid*. Ovid's main technique here is to avoid competing directly, sliding over the 'famous' parts by compressing them into a few lines. So the tale of Dido and Aeneas, probably the best-known portion of the *Aeneid*, which occupies all of Book 4 and portions of Books 1, 2, and 6, gets four lines from Ovid (*Met.* 14.78–81).

On the other hand, Ovid expands a moment in the *Aeneid* where Aeneas and his men run into Achaemenides (abandoned by Odysseus in the Cyclops's cave) and take him on board. Ovid adds another Odyssean castaway, Macareus, who questions Achaemenides about his Trojan companions and hears a more up-to-date version of their story. The net effect of this insertion into the text is to undermine Vergil: the *Aeneid* had appeared to offer a seamless narrative of the past, incorporating Homer as a way to show its veracity, but now we see (Ovid's suggestion of) Vergil's intrusive hand, selecting only certain bits of the story (see Section 2.1 on Ovid's interest in how stories are told). All storytellers do this, of course, especially when they are working with traditional material, but through his use of telling detail and allusions toward what is omitted, Ovid often makes it seem as if his predecessors have missed a trick, either through incompetence or some more subversive motive.

Ovid's relationship to Vergil is a special one; Vergil lived in the generation immediately prior to Ovid's, and was, during his lifetime, the most famous poet at Rome. Ovid is often called Vergil's 'best reader', and his view of Vergil is a tendentious one. Most of the time, he does not quote directly from Vergil, but when he does, it is with telling, often deflationary, effect. For instance, when Aeneas is headed to the underworld, he is told that going down is easy, but *hoc opus, hic labor est* ('here is the work, here is the effort', *Aeneid* 6.129), namely to return to the mortal sphere. Ovid quotes these words exactly, in *Ars* 1.453, where he is instructing the student that *his* effort should be spent getting the *puella* into bed without giving her a present first. To refer to such a tense moment in Vergil, pregnant with historical import, in the context of seduction is cheeky beyond belief, and characteristically Ovidian.

Ovid's reuse of the Greco-Roman literary tradition is too sophisticated to be covered by the term 'pastiche'; so too, it would not quite be accurate to call this parody, at least not as the term is normally understood. Parody and pastiche tend to be merely imitative, sometimes even destructive, but Ovid generally creates far more than he destroys.

Revision

Beyond 'recycling' other people's material, Ovid also regularly engaged in revision of his own work; this is one of the reasons his poetry is so difficult to date (see Section 1.1 on chronology). He wrote, he tells us, two editions of *Amores*, trimming five books to three; the 'single' *Heroides* engendered a 'double' set (possibly at the suggestion of a friend; *Am.* 2.18.27–34); *Ars* 3 markets itself as a necessary coda to *Ars* 1 and 2, and the trilogy is then further modified by the addition of the *Remedia*; the *Fasti* and *Metamorphoses* are contemporaneous retellings of a number of the same stories, each reusing set scenes from amatory works; the *Fasti* itself bears two prologues (1.3–26 and 2.15–18), suggesting revision in exile to appeal to a new patron; there are two collections of exile poetry. *Tristia* 1.1.119–20 (playfully?) suggests a new ending to the *Metamorphoses* which incorporates the poet's own final, disastrous change of identity.

In addition to formal revision of completed poems, Ovid also engages in a number of forms of generic and thematic revisiting. His earliest works, the *Heroides* and *Amores*, treat of topics which are themselves perhaps rather circumscribed: love elegy is usually the outpourings of a male poet at the cruel behaviour of his withholding *puella*, and its practitioners pace relentlessly over the same small space of unhappy love. So too, the women (and men) of the *Heroides* are in fact rather different from one another, but they regularly use the same vocabulary and imagery to bemoan their fates; it is almost as if Ovid were trying to work out a typology of all that could be said in a particular amatory situation, and indeed, the *Heroides* were taken by some later readers precisely as epistolary models. Ovid also regularly 'contaminates' his other poetry with elegiac themes and language – both the *Metamorphoses* and the *Fasti* abound with the kinds of love stories previously covered in the amatory poetry – and for that matter, the *Amores, Heroides,* and *Ars Amatoria* also inserted a variety of mythological narratives of the kind which might seem more appropriate to mythological or historical-religious works such as epic.

Recent scholarship has argued that the various kinds of Ovidian repetition are not an unfortunate tick of the poet which we should ignore or explain away, but rather, the single most distinctive and influential feature of his compositional style. Indeed, the poetry revels in its inability to be pinned down, its own 'metamorphic' qualities. We might see Ovid as deliberately setting puzzles for the reader to solve, such as whether the second edition of the *Amores* was only, as it suggests, a slimming-down, or whether new poems were added, or whether Ovid really did start work on a grand epic about the battles of gods and giants (see Section 2.1). It is probably anachronistic to consider this effect deliberate (contemporary readers might well have had a copy of the first edition of the *Amores*), but one result that might be more intentional is that Ovid's poetry always has a dynamic feel. We are never certain we have the last word: for instance, is it coincidence that so many of the stories in *Met.* 2 and 3 focus on seeing things one should not, and on the virtues of keeping one's mouth shut, given that Ovid will tell us that one of the causes of his relegation was seeing something he should not have seen (see Section 3.2)? In a rather different vein, Ovid regularly 'advertises' one poem in another, as when *Amores* 2.18 and *Ars* 3 tout the *Heroides* and the *Ars* suggests the *Amores* as handy to get you 'in the mood', or when *Remedia* 71–2 claims that just as reading Ovid got you in love, so reading Ovid will get you out of it. By referring to his own previous writings so consistently, Ovid seems to place himself in the category of his famous predecessors, and simultaneously makes an 'Augustan' point; the emperor also posits himself as an exemplar to others.

There is another, less obvious feature to Ovidian repetition, one we have already noticed (see Section 2.1). This is the fact that in telling the same story Ovid often does so with a difference each time. One well-known example is the series of rapes in the first two books of the *Metamorphoses*, each of which is more or less the same (god sees nymph, god chases nymph, god rapes nymph) – but in fact, the variation on the basic theme renders each story unique. In the first, Apollo chases the nymph Daphne, but before he catches her, she prays to her father, a river, and is changed into a bay tree. Then Jupiter rapes Io, daughter of a river-god, but the untimely appearance of his wife means that he has to turn his victim into a heifer, which he then gives to Juno. Suspicious – as she might well be – Juno assigns a guardian, the hundred-eyed Argos. Jupiter begins to feel guilty, and so he sends Mercury to kill Argos and free Io, a feat which Mercury accomplishes by telling Argos the story of Pan's attempted rape of the nymph Syrinx. Pan fails because Syrinx is changed into reed pipes (which is what her name means in Greek). The story, not so different from the two we have just heard, puts Argos to sleep. In addition to serving as a warning to the reader, potentially bored by the same topic, to pay attention, the overall effect is similar to the authenticating gestures of the *Amores* in light of the *Ars*; we see, through the relentless repetition, that gods are likely to be rapists. In fact, a number of the female characters in the first third of the poem seem also to have 'learned' this fact – more often than not, they simply see a god and break into a run!

In addition to serving as the passive recipient of repetitive tales, sometimes the reader is more directly drawn into the repetition. For instance, we are often provided with two different interpretations of an event or a story. Not only does the teacher of the *Ars* offer advice he cannot take (see Section 2.1), which destabilizes his authority, but individual narrators in the *Metamorphoses* provide radically different interpretations of the world. For example, Achelous the river-god tells in *Met.* 8 a story of how a girl he loved was changed into an island, whereupon Pirithous (son of the notoriously impious Ixion) objects that these things do not happen in real life, that Achelous 'makes the gods too powerful, if they can give and take forms away' (*Met.* 8.614– 15). The rest of the audience, Ovid tells us, is shocked (it is not clear whether they disagree or simply find him rude), especially Lelex, who tells a story of metamorphosis, caused by the gods as a reward for good behaviour. After this story, told at some length, we hear that Theseus was interested in hearing more (an intertextual joke, as Lelex's story is similar to a Callimachean poem featuring Theseus), but Achelous changes the subject, to gods who, like himself, are shape-shifters. There

Fig. 5 Correggio, Jupiter and Io.

is no return to the question of which man is correct – presumably, the *Metamorphoses* as a whole, in which gods *do* give and take forms away, tends to support Lelex's view – but Pirithous's response is certainly left available to the reader, who might consider all that comes before and after as mere fiction. And the majority of the poem's metamorphoses are *not* attributed to a god. Or perhaps we might see this as Ovid's way of incorporating the reader who is less prone to enter into the spirit of the text by creating her analogue within the poem (but note that such a reader must also, implicitly, accept the characterization as impious).

Repetition and Repetitiveness

Such complex questions about narrative pose more of a problem for the professional than the amateur, who may not be bothered by them, however interesting they are in their own right. But even a casual reader is likely to be struck by Ovid's interest in exploring a topic from many different angles (for many centuries, this was dismissively thought of as 'repetitiveness'). Previous generations saw the *Heroides* as depressingly similar, and the exile poetry as similarly harping on one topic at excessive length. The *Amores,* as we have noted, can indeed seem at first look like a meticulous checklist of themes from a previous elegy, dutifully treated. But there is more: Ovid regularly returns to particular stories or individuals for inspiration (e.g. three Medeas: *Heroides* 12, the lost tragedy and *Met.* 7). And Ovid, from exile, writes himself into the tales of several of his abandoned heroines, and fashions himself as a new Odysseus. Some readers find Ovid's reuse of material delightful, others wearying.

There are two main effects of Ovidian recycling, revision and repetition. The first, and simpler, is that they somewhat paradoxically give an impression of exuberant superabundance, in part because of the multiple variations on each basic theme or character. While repetition can sometimes hint at a dearth of ideas, Ovid's *copia* ('abundant supply') is everywhere apparent. This is perhaps best encapsulated by the example of rape (again). Arachne's tapestry in *Met.* 6 (see Section 3.2) dizzyingly lists rapes committed by the gods in various guises, twenty-one of them in twenty-four lines (6.103–26); most of them simply list the rapist's name as the subject and the woman's name as the direct object. The first five books had already told fourteen narratives of rape and attempted rape (these are among the most vivid tales of the poem), and had included, as we have noted, an object lesson in the middle of the third one, about the importance of paying attention even when you have heard the story before, lest you lose your head. By Book 6, we have given up wondering how many more of these stories the narrator has; perhaps we are curious as to whether he can continue to vary them; perhaps we are disturbed by the theme. But then, in one fell swoop, Arachne uses up the leftovers: thereafter the poem stops telling stories of rape (more or less; there are a few more, and the *Fasti* also includes several). So it becomes clear that the narrator of the poem is not carefully doling out a limited store of mythic material; instead he is flaunting the infinite variety at his disposal by throwing handfuls at us. The *Ibis* also makes this clear; as noted earlier, Ovid alludes in it to dozens of mythical stories we know, but also to quite a number unattested elsewhere in extant literature.

The more complicated effect of such systematic repetition is that the world of poetry and the real world become blurred (the 'reality effect', whereby fiction takes on the qualities of life). Ovid's play on the border between truth and fiction is marked, but also authenticated; the reader is more likely to find Ovid's sometimes fanciful claims plausible from having heard them 'somewhere' before. This happens most evidently in the *Ars*, which rework a number of incidents in the *Amores* (see Section 2.1 on the beating-the-*puella* incident of *Am.* 1.7). Among many examples, *Ars* 1.575–8 suggests drinking from the same part of the cup as one's lover as a sign of affection, which Ovid himself had done at *Am.* 1.4.31.4 (and which Paris will do in *Her.* 16.255–6, varying the trope by kissing Helen's daughter after she does). Quite a number of the 'real-life stories' of the *Ars* are also mythological, which adds a distancing layer – or does it bring them closer? These stories, whether made up by Ovid or part of traditional mythology, seem intended to provide evidence for the effectiveness of the instruction of the *Ars*; it is more often the case that they fail spectacularly.

Repetition of various kinds constitutes a key feature of Ovid's style. For many generations of critics, this was a flaw. More recently, it has been understood as contributing to Ovid's style as a whole, and especially his interest in how narrators affect the stories they tell, and in the political implications of who tells what (see Section 3.3). We will notice later, in Section 3.2, that Ovid seems to offer a theory of repetition in his tale of Echo. So too, repetition and revision work together in a more complicated way in the case of the *Ars* and the *Amores*: noticing that the *Ars* authenticates itself via the *Amores* may prompt us to re-read the earlier collection. If we do engage in a second reading, we cannot help but notice that the narrator we grew increasingly suspicious of during our first reading has now fully revealed himself to be nothing but a charlatan: what looked like progressive but honest disillusionment with Corinna turns out to be the carefully planned out stages of a game (a lesson, even) which repeats endlessly, each time with a new female victim (see Section 2.1 for discussion of how successive poems in the *Amores* can also cause readers to revise as they read). To be sure, even in the *Amores* there was more than one girl, but we might have seen that as the poet's defence against Corinna's typically elegiac behaviour. Now we know, or know more certainly, that she could have been any woman at all, that this was always how the story was going to end.

Our focus on the marginality of Ovid's own self-positioning may have obscured the key fact that he has been, for two millennia, a much-loved and much-imitated poet. He was (perhaps surprisingly) a standard schoolroom text all across Europe for hundreds of years, and was alternately a treasure-trove for artists and a scapegoat for moralists. To do justice to the influence of Ovid on later poets, visual artists and composers would need a volume many times the size of this one. From Chaucer to James Joyce, Titian to Picasso, Mozart to Bob Dylan – a hundred more names could be added – each generation has found something slightly different to value in the poetry of Ovid. The later Middle Ages and early Renaissance were especially interested in him, and contemporaries sometimes call our own times another 'age of Ovid', in which his poetry and worldview have come to be seen as touching upon our own most pressing concerns. Some of why that is should by now be obvious: his vivid ability to paint a lush word picture, for instance, makes him an excellent choice for painters, and his explorations of the working of power also make him feel very modern.

I focus for a moment on a single piece of the vast picture of Ovid's poetic afterlife, that strand of the tradition (deriving ultimately from his influence on medieval troubadour or 'courtly' culture) which sees Ovid as *the* poet of love, especially love for its own sake (i.e. often outside of the context of marriage). Taken out of their Roman context, his amatory poems fit into and help to create a turn toward eroticism, especially in its hidden and ironic manifestations. The alternation between denial and fulfilment instantiated in Ovid's love poetry was distilled into its essence, eventually to become a kind of amatory code, with the *puella* transmuted into the chaste love object (Dante's Beatrice and Petrarch's Laura are the two most famous from this period, but there are many others, including – with further alterations – Shakespeare's 'dark lady' and beyond). For some, Ovid's biography was an important part of the story, as it traced the path from sexual adventurer to 'serious' poet who suffered for his art, and even, in some versions of his tale, to Christian convert. In this, one of the many metamorphoses of Ovid's poetry through the ages, we can see his infinite susceptibility to repetitive gestures.

3

Romans at Home and Abroad: Identity and the Colonial Subject

3.1 Strangers in a Strange Land: Explorers and Exiles

This section focuses on Ovid's habit of peopling his poetry with narratives of individuals out of place, taken away from the familiar. These groups of people fall into two basic categories. What they have in common is that all are depicted as displaced persons. Some are temporarily so: wanderers or explorers, unwitting adventurers who find themselves away from home (or, to expand our metaphor, merely in a new situation; sometimes the 'voyage' is one of discovery). Others are permanent outcasts, forced out of their homes for a variety of reasons, or even suffering from profound alienation right in their own backyards. The first group includes many of Ovid's main storytellers, reporting what they have unearthed on their journeys, like the poet's personae in the *Ars* or the *Fasti*, or quite a number of narrators in the *Metamorphoses*. The second group, people who are permanently in transition, or who no longer have a home, includes mythical city-founders such as Cadmus and Aeneas, and the wily Medea (who escapes town just in time to avoid punishment for her crimes, thrice), but also less historically significant figures such as slaves, forcibly displaced from their homes. And, of course, Ovid himself eventually becomes the most fully fleshed-out of these characters in exile; only with his death does he move from the 'temporary' into the 'permanent' category of wanderers.

Adventurers

Perseus, featured in *Met.* 4 and 5, is a good example of a temporary wanderer, although the poem is full of them. Exiled by his grandfather because of his illegitimate birth, he acquires a series of special powers. These include a set of wings which allow him to fly, and the decapitated head of the Gorgon Medusa, which has the power to turn anyone who meets its gaze to stone. Unlike many of Ovid's adventurers, Perseus is not much of a storyteller. Instead, he flits about, affecting the world in ways large and small: while he is flying over Libya, drops of gore from Medusa's head land in the desert, and are changed into the snakes for which the area is notorious (4.616–20). He flies all over the known world, and eventually makes his way to the Ethiopians, where he discovers the lovely Andromeda, chained to a rock and soon to be eaten by a monster. He might simply petrify the monster, but, lest he seem unheroic, or like a man who can succeed only through magic tricks, he instead does battle with it and eventually emerges triumphant. (While he is cleaning up afterward, he puts the Gorgon's head on a bed of seaweed, whence we have coral, pliant underwater but hard above it.) He marries Andromeda but her uncle, to whom she had been engaged, breaks up the wedding feast. A battle ensues, in which Perseus is ultimately victorious thanks to the Gorgon's head (and he even creates, as he observes, sculptures to decorate the palace!). He then returns home with his bride, and lives happily ever after.

The figure of Perseus as Ovid portrays him is rather different from how he is traditionally presented. First, the poet focuses on the sheer joy of Perseus's ability to travel from place to place; he is a tourist, rather than an exile, flitting about seeing the sights. Second, and despite the fact that he does eventually 'get the girl', Ovid seems to emphasize the faintly unheroic nature of his behaviour. Perseus kills Medusa in order to obtain the spoil of her head, but does so by literally refusing to face her (he uses his shield as a reflector to see where she is), and the story of his theft of the single eye of the Graiae – three old women, spooky but hardly a real challenge – is given just as many lines, suggesting its equal importance in understanding him. So too, Perseus performs brave acts:

the fight-scene in *Met.* 5 is about as close as the poem comes to giving us a standard epic battle-narrative. But when he realizes that 'his strength would be defeated by the crowd' (5.177), he pulls out the Gorgon's head and turns the remainder of his enemies to stone. Perseus is, then, a kind of 'colonizing' wanderer, who explores the world to see what it can offer him (see Section 3.3).

Ovid has regular recourse to such deflationary tactics when he deals with traditional kinds of heroes. Other wanderers in the *Metamorphoses*, however, receive a friendlier treatment, especially when they are also storytellers (see Section 3.2 for Ovid's interest in artists both literary and plastic). We have already mentioned Macareus and Achaemenides, repurposed from their travels in Homer to tell their stories anew. And Orpheus, the mythic singer of *Met.* 10, voyages to the underworld to persuade its rulers to allow his wife to live again after she has been fatally bitten by a snake. He is ultimately successful, and she returns with him. Only there is a catch: he had been ordered not to look at her before reaching the surface; his last-minute weakening of will means that he loses her forever. Despite the fact that Orpheus is clearly to blame for this failing, the narrator treats him with a great deal of sympathy.

In a number of works, Ovid takes on the role of 'knowledgeable voyager' himself; this happens, for instance, in the *Fasti*, when he quizzes various gods about the things he wants to know (see Section 2.1 on the month of June). Here he is a bold adventurer, summoning up his courage to open up new frontiers of knowledge, even if, as happens especially with constellations, he gets the information wrong! So too, in the *Ars*, he details his hard-won experience with women, including frank assessments of what did and did not work for him (and *Ars* 3 proceeds to 'arm the Amazons', in a gesture which shows the teacher's dedication to his subject, even when it will disadvantage him personally). Even the *Amores* could fall into this category, if we see the lover as a sexual adventurer, documenting erotic exotica (3.7, a poem about Ovid's impotence, presents the poet as a speaker of truth, even where it is unflattering; 2.10 describes Ovid as – horrifyingly! – in love with two women at once – but willing to give it his best effort).

Eventually, Ovid literally becomes a wanderer, and narrates strange tales from the edge of the world. For – as may not yet have become clear – the exile poetry is not simply full of lament and complaint. It also contains quite a lot of (fictionalized) travel narrative. *Tr.* 3.9 fancifully derives the name of Tomis from the Greek verb *temno*, to cut, and tells the story of Medea's dismemberment of her brother and scattering the pieces in the ocean: her father stopped to collect his body, and thus Medea and Jason were able to make their escape. Ovid also provides other 'Scythian tales', describing the exiled priestess Iphigeneia's near-sacrifice of her brother Orestes (*EP* 3.2). And *Tr.* 3.10, along with other poems, offers a full-blown description of the horrors Ovid suffers and the strange customs he witnesses. Ovid-in-exile is emphatically not a tourist, but his letters from the topsy-turvy world of Tomis make clear that he is a traveller who keeps his eyes open and is willing and able to weave the material of daily life into stories that he can tell others. Further, the questionable truth-value of a number of his claims (see Section 2.1), poses the question to what extent his voyage is a mental one.

Refugees

Our second group of outsiders in Ovid's poetry is those who find themselves more permanently displaced. The figure of Evander, who flees Arcadia in Greece with his mother, at her prophetic warning of danger, is depicted briefly in *Fas.* 1.471–98. He is rather an ordinary man, and to cheer him up his mother explains that he is exiled through no fault of his own: 'you are pushed out of the city by an offended god' (*Fas.* 1.482). She then reminds him of a variety of other exiles, and that exalted company elevates his mood, such that he sails to Italy and settles in nicely. It is probably not over-reading to see something of the exilic Ovid in the figure of Evander; as we noted in Section 1.1, the first two books of the *Fasti* bear signs of revision in exile, and the vocabulary used here is just how Ovid refers to his own removal from Rome.

A number of Ovid's exiles have larger roles to play. Pythagoras, who gets to deliver the longest single speech in the *Metamorphoses* (15.75–478), is in voluntary exile from Samos. His speech has been read as offering a microcosm of the poem, for his cosmogony complements and expands upon that offered in Book 1, and his philosophy, which can be summarized by the notion that everything is in flux, can be supported by certain interpretations of the poem. But, as is regularly the case in the *Metamorphoses*, the pieces do not fit: his speech begins and ends by urging vegetarianism (the feature of the Pythagorean sect that was most ridiculed in antiquity, however respectable it now appears). And his list of great cities that have risen and fallen ends with Rome, though he remains silent about its eventual fate. We might regard him as a wisdom figure, but he is one whose claims to knowledge are undermined; even within the poem we are told that his words are not believed by his audience.

Some of the mythological women of the *Heroides* are also permanent exiles. Ariadne and Medea (authors of *Her.* 10 and 12 respectively) have each left home, and done so in such a way that return would not be easy, since they have betrayed their families to elope with handsome strangers. Dido (*Her.* 7) was an exile before Aeneas came along, since her brother forced her out of her kingdom, but she seems to feel her isolation all the more because she (mistakenly) thought she had found a partner to share in it. Hermione, author of *Heroides* 8, there – uniquely – presents herself as a kidnap victim snatched away from her family.

Of all of these figures, Medea best repays a closer look, because Ovid returned to her character repeatedly. As we have noted (see Section 2.2), Medea is above all an intertextual heroine, whose story has been told over and over again. So, slight differences are important, as they indicate larger divergences below the surface. *Her.* 12 presents a Medea who has already been abandoned; she begins by focusing on her regrets about the past. But she soon rehearses how Jason placed himself at her mercy, and then details the various crimes she committed for him. Then, in a dramatic development, she explains that their child has just seen Jason in (what she knows is) a wedding procession. She begs Jason to return to her, but her own anger seeps through her final lines. In the beginning of *Met.* 7, by contrast, we catch Medea at an earlier life-stage; she has only just met Jason. She struggles with her feelings for him, but eventually gives in, apparently in full knowledge of how things will turn out ('I see what I am doing, nor is it ignorance of the truth which will trick me, but love', 7.92–3). The narrative then focuses more closely upon her deeds of magic – and crime – and ends with an extremely abbreviated rendition of the infanticide.

Ovid's first extended portrayal of Medea concentrates upon the isolation and powerlessness which are characteristic of exilic figures in Ovid. But each of his narratives also makes clear the terrifying kind of power that can come from being an outcast; in the first, Medea's anger is something to be feared, and in the second, the telling of her astounding deeds gains in import from their matter-of-fact narration. The deeds of Medea, and a number of other exiles in Ovid, make clear that the position of the exile is not merely one of powerlessness.

There are also a number of less-exalted figures in Ovid's poetry who are forced out of their homes, and one primary category into which they fall is prisoners of war and slaves. While Ovid presents himself as actively uninterested in war and the military life (except in its metaphorical, 'love-is-just-like-war' elegiac incarnation, as in *Am.* 1.9), he is certainly willing to benefit from the fruits of empire. We have already discussed Briseis, the author of *Her.* 3, as a figure who destabilizes the stories of epic (see Section 2.1); she also provides an example of a prisoner of war, enslaved and sharing the bed of her captor who, as she herself reminds us, killed her father and three brothers when he sacked Lyrnessos (*Her.* 3.45–56). So too, we have discussed Cypassis, the hair-dressing slave of the *Amores*, permanently at the disposal of her Roman masters (see Section 3.2 for more on Ovidian slaves).

Just as temporary voyaging can serve as a metaphor for the quest for knowledge in Ovid, so too, permanent exile can be expanded to encompass a profound isolation that need not require physical movement. Ovidian tales of metamorphosis often include a moment where bodily alteration is first realized and the self becomes alienated. In some cases, people changed into animals haunt family members, hoping to be recognized by them; such is the case with Io, who, having been raped by Jupiter and then changed into a cow, writes her name with her hoof (it is lucky for her that her name is only two letters long, and convenient for Ovid that '*io*' is Greek for 'woe is me'!). Her father does understand this communication, but it does not comfort him much. Callisto, raped by Jupiter and turned into a bear, sees her son and attempts, fruitlessly, to communicate with him. Not unnaturally, he does not recognize his mother in this form, and very nearly kills her, saved only by the intervention of Jupiter, who turns them both into constellations. It is surely part of the trauma of both women to discover that their very identities are unstable: each is simultaneously human and animal, able to recognize family members but not to maintain a relationship with them. Philomela too is removed from her homeland before she suffers rape and mutilation. Ovid typically does not encourage the reader to pause over these moments of poignancy, rushing on to tell another story, but they stand out in re-readings of the poem. Among other things, metamorphosis nearly always means exile: even Io, eventually turned back into human form, lives out the rest of her life in a foreign land.

This returns us to the exilic figure of Ovid himself. Because of his lifelong habit of revision (see Section 2.2), we cannot always be sure how his own biography influenced individual depictions of exiles. Indeed, the fact that a favoured metaphorical trope became literal is only partly ironic: in a manner eerily similar to one of his own characters, Ovid-the-outsider eventually occupies a borderland, revealing characteristics that had before lain dormant. Or perhaps there is no irony, and Augustus was a cleverer reader than Ovid gave him credit for: one response to a poet who always locates himself on the margins is to take him at his word. (Quite a number of modern Ovid novels play with this notion, such as David Malouf's 1978 *An Imaginary Life* and Christoph Ransmyer's 1988 *The Last World*.)

Perhaps disturbingly, the figure of the outsider was of enormous interest to Ovid even before life imitated art. And – as generations of anthropologists have discovered – it is often only from a position simultaneously inside and outside that one can understand a behaviour, or a culture. The place where we see the majority of our explorers is, of course, the *Metamorphoses*, whose major theme is change. In fact, it has been suggested that the 'hero' of the poem is change itself, or perhaps, the god Chaos. Although change is a constant, human beings like to have unexpected changes explained, and storytelling is one of our main methods of explanation. So a great many of the aetiological ('where-things-came-from') tales in the poem fall into this category of knowledgeable people explaining things, sometimes in direct speech, and sometimes with Ovid as the implied narrator.

We have already noticed the heated scholarly debate about what to make of the persona Ovid presents to us in his exile poetry. On the surface, he is powerless, miserable, grovelling for forgiveness. *He* is the foreigner, forced to rely upon savages for his every need. On the other hand, it is also in the exile poetry that Ovid comes to see his own power: we find here his boldest claims to poetic immortality. So the power that comes from being at the margin is also visible here. Perhaps Ovid is the affable but quotidian Evander, or perhaps he is better seen as a menacing Medea-figure, continuing to do magic with words. But he surely possesses more power and more authority than he often suggests is the case.

3.2 Speaking and Silence: Victims and Victimizers

Speech and Punishment

We have already noticed Ovid's interest in the kinds of stories people tell. Here we focus on the two intertwined themes of speaking and (coerced) silence, and the examination of unequal power relations which underpins many of Ovid's narratives. As we shall see, it would not be unfair to call these the basic themes of much of Ovid's poetry; even where they are not his explicit subject, they crop up with distressing frequency (as, for instance, in the very title of the *Fasti*, which refers to days on which business can be conducted, but literally means 'days which can be spoken (about)'). And it is perhaps precisely his self-appointed role as outsider that makes Ovid so well suited to noticing who is allowed to say what to whom.

Ovid tells many stories about the effects of speech, or, more broadly, communicative attempts in general. He seems especially concerned with occasions where speech proves dangerous for the speaker. Quite a number of characters are literally shut up because they either have said, or might say, something others want kept silent. We have already looked briefly at the story of Tereus's grotesque silencing of his rape victim Philomela, and at Io's effective but still hampered attempt to name herself. The story of the nymph Lara in *Fas*. 2 is similar, but with a twist: Lara is first silenced, by Juno, because she used to prattle and so distract the goddess from her husband's affairs, and then raped by Mercury because she cannot object: 'he prepared to rape her, and she pleaded with him with her expression instead of words; in vain, she tried to speak with her mute tongue' (2.613–14). So too, we might notice in *Met*. 2 the tale of the centaur (half-woman, half-horse) Ocyrhoe, who, while uttering a prophecy better left unspoken, is silenced by the unusual expedient of being changed entirely into a horse.

Other examples abound, but one of the most compelling is the story of Echo, similar to Lara's but much better-known. We noted (see Section 2.1; *Met*. 3.359–401) that the beautiful but self-involved Narcissus was courted by many. One of them was the nymph Echo, who, like Lara, used to distract Juno while Jupiter was frolicking on the mountainside. Juno punishes her not by removing her power of speech, but by enabling her only to repeat what is said to her. Luckily for her, she happens to be following Narcissus when he finds himself alone and seeking his companions; he speaks out loud just the words she herself would like to use (Ovid is here at his wittiest; the sexual nuances of Echo's responses are deliberate): 'Is someone here?' 'Here!' 'Come!'

'Come!' 'Why do you run away from me?' 'Why do you run away from me?' 'Here, let's come together!' 'Let's come together!' At this point, feeling suitably encouraged, Echo runs to embrace him, and in response to his outraged 'Over my dead body I'll give you all I've got!' returns 'I'll give you all I've got!' She runs away in shame, and eventually dissolves, retaining only a disembodied voice. There is much to be said about Echo in relation to Ovidian repetition: she, like the poet, manages to use the same old words in strikingly different ways. Still – and perhaps in an unintentional foreshadowing of the Ovidian biography – while Echo retains her identity, she is seemingly deprived of the power to effect any change in the world.

Shortly before this story, Ovid narrates the tale of Actaeon. We have already noticed the way Ovid plays with the notions of presence and absence in Actaeon's story (see Section 2.1; *Met.* 3.155–252); here we focus on his silencing. Actaeon, a hunter, is out in the forest with a group of friends (and dogs). He happens to wander into a grotto where the virgin goddess Diana is bathing with her nymphs; they try to hide her from his sight but, Ovid says, she is so much taller than they that their attempts are ineffective. Diana wishes she had her arrows to hand, but, since she does not, she throws water into the hunter's face, saying 'go ahead and tell that you have seen me without my clothes on – if you *can* tell!' Actaeon is thus turned into a deer, and mauled by his own dogs, with his friends looking on and unknowingly cheering his destruction. This story is especially interesting for its Ovidian afterlife: first, in a rare description of the effect of a story, the narrator tells us that there was much debate about whether Diana's behaviour was crueller than necessary, or an appropriate defence of her virginity. (Presumably, it will not matter much to Actaeon either way.) Even more interestingly, *Tr.* 2, which contains some of Ovid's earliest reflections upon his exile, compares himself to Actaeon (2.103–6): 'Why did I see something? Why did I make my eyes accomplices? Why was a fault recognized by foolish me? Actaeon innocently saw Diana without her clothing; still, he became the prize for his own dogs!' It is, of course, possible that Ovid revised the earlier parts of the *Metamorphoses* to reflect his own

Fig. 6 Cesari, Diana and Actaeon.

biography, but this is not a necessary conclusion, as much of his work obsessively returns to this theme. Perhaps this is not art reflecting life, but instead exile is a confirmation of Ovid's worst fears: somebody *was* listening, and decided to shut him up.

Such object lessons about the dangers of communication concentrate particularly in Ovid's stories of artists. Art is, of course, a form of communication, and Ovid's poetry seems especially interested in places where that communication either fails, or succeeds to its own detriment. The *Metamorphoses* is full of tales of what happens to those whose art challenges authority figures: the singer Orpheus of *Met.* 10, who persuades the underworld gods to give him his wife back, but unfortunately turns around to see that she is safe, and so loses her; Marsyas of *Met.* 6, who challenges Apollo to a singing contest, loses, and is flayed alive; the Pierides, a group of sisters who challenge the Muses to a singing contest in *Met.* 5, lose, and are turned into chattering magpies; perhaps even Niobe of the many offspring, who in *Met.* 6 boasts one time too many that her 'work' is far superior to the production of Leto, who has given birth to only two children, Apollo and Artemis, and is then forced to watch as the dynamic duo kills every one of her dozen. Such figures are generally unappreciated, and often punished. On the other hand, they are also often boastful, and deserve to be taken down a peg – so it is perhaps over-simplistic to see them simply as avatars of Ovid; he rather uses them to explore a variety of relationships between artist and audience.

The most notable artist figure of the *Metamorphoses*, and of Ovid's work as a whole, is Pygmalion. He is a sculptor who, disgusted by the unchaste behaviour of the local women, decides to remain celibate. He fashions the perfect woman out of ivory, and then falls in love with it/her; thanks to his well-received prayer to a friendly Venus, he then feels her/it come to life under his own hands. They live happily ever after (but their great-granddaughter Myrrha falls in love with and is impregnated by her own father – the poem does not draw any connection between the two events, although many readers do). There is quite a lot going on in this tale, and critics have pointed to the Ovidian way in which Pygmalion's life imitates his art, the fact that his superb artistry is used to create a luxury item for private consumption, the creepiness (but also the profound 'elegiac-ness') of being able to fashion one's ideal woman, the disturbing but also natural act of falling in love with one's own creation, and the generations-later punishment which we might or might not want to see as a result of Pygmalion's abnormal behaviour. Here again, Ovid does not provide us with a clear moral, or even an interpretation.

There are many other Ovidian artists, but the weaver Arachne is another extremely significant one. She is a low-born craftswoman who seeks to transcend her condition by her art and challenges Minerva to a weaving contest. Her topic, as we have already seen, is the deceptive forms the gods take to deceive and rape mortal women (a strange topic for a young woman, but she is deliberately conveying a message to Minerva about her divine relatives). Much scholarly ink has been spilt on the tapestries made by the two women; Minerva's is 'classical', with a single, main topic (her own defeat of Neptune in a competition about

Fig. 7 Rodin, Pygmalion and Galatea.

who will be the patron god of Athens), described in such a way that it might be visually replicated, with a neat border around it. Arachne's, by contrast, is, like the *Metamorphoses* itself, wild, undisciplined, full of detail, perhaps even 'baroque'. Interestingly, the poem cannot quite bring itself to declare a winner: 'Not Athena [= Minerva], nor Envy herself would have been able to pick the work apart. The blonde goddess

Fig. 8 Houasse, Minerve et Arachne.

was pained at Arachne's success' (*Met.* 6.129–30). And Minerva's
reaction is to beat Arachne senseless; Arachne responds by trying to
hang herself and, in pity, Minerva turns her into a spider (Greek
'arachnid'). This familiar story-pattern in the *Metamorphoses*, in which
a mortal offends a god, either wittingly or unwittingly, and then suffers
a brutal punishment, may be mitigated by Minerva's metamorphosis.
Or perhaps it merely serves as further punishment: some observe that
Arachne still has her art, others that the work of spiders is repetitive and
without creativity.

Female and Other Victims

Our brief study of artists has focused on the ways individuals with
power use and abuse it, and how those on the margins are often simply
victimized without any recourse to justice. Ovid regularly treats us to
the unedifying spectacle of naked power, which sometimes deigns to
cloak itself, and this 'peeling away' of covering narratives to show

coercion underneath invites a number of responses. Indeed, some scholars see this exposure of the workings of authority as a main theme of Augustan literature, which is not surprising given that the balance of power in the real world was shifting in unpredictable ways, and that one individual in particular was quietly reshaping the world according to his will.

On the one hand, especially in the *Metamorphoses*, Ovid regularly identifies with victims, and portrays them with a surprising degree of sympathy. On the other hand, in the *Amores* the Ovidian persona is himself regularly a perpetrator of injustice against others (see Section 2.1), which makes this sympathy seem paradoxical. Like other elegists, but more brazenly, Ovid manages to have it both ways, simultaneously enjoying his dominance over others and suggesting that he is the kind of person who feels the sufferings of others deeply (even when he is their cause). But this may be an unfair assessment: those who are genuinely victimized sometimes do lash out, trying to effect change in any way they can from within the system that entraps them. Either way (and these two positions do not exhaust the possibilities), many readers find the disjunction between Ovid's compassion and his exploitation profoundly disturbing.

For instance, feminist, or female, readers of Ovid cannot help but notice that women are a primary category of those victimized within the poetry; we have already treated numerous rapes casually, in passing (as, usually, does Ovid himself). Ovid's poetry is too rich to summarize any aspect of it in a sentence, but it is not entirely unfair to characterize women's roles in it by saying that they normally serve as the objects of men's desire and dominance. First-time readers of the *Metamorphoses*, especially the opening five books, are nearly always struck by the prevalence of rape as a narrative tool, and the principle holds throughout, except in the exile poetry. Sometimes, as in *Am.* 1.5, women are fetishized; more often they are used and discarded (we might remember again Cypassis, Corinna's slave/hairdresser, see Sections 1.1 and 2.1). So too, scholars have long noted the ways in which the *puella* of elegy becomes a metaphor for the poetry itself, and for the Muse which inspires it: Ovid explicitly suggests that the *puella* 'offer yourself to me, happy material for my poetry', *Am.* 1.3.19, but the notion is implicit throughout his poetry, and influential on the women who people the poetry of many of his successors.

The equation between woman and poetic material helps to explain, even if it does not render more palatable, the voyeuristic way in which women in Ovid's poetry are often portrayed (film theory's notion of the 'male gaze' and the ways in which this desire to look can contaminate or implicate the viewer/reader have been fruitfully applied to a number of Ovidian scenes). So in *Am.* 1.14 when Ovid criticizes Corinna for over-dyeing her hair – it has fallen out! – he is also staking a metapoetic claim about the use of artifice and trickery in literature: the simple style is best. For many scholars, this helps to explain the lopsided portraits we are given of elegiac mistresses – they are 'real' in an even more contingent way than most characters in fiction, because they are fulfilling a number of functions at once.

There are a number of explanations for Ovid's pose in the *Amores* as a playboy, despite his explicit claim that he is not a *desultor amoris* ('hop-on, hop-off lover', *Am.* 1.3.15). One of the reasons the *Amores* boasts so much about the different women Ovid has slept with (slightly irregular for elegy) may be to allow the poet to play upon the regular notion of woman as 'unexplored territory'; this makes its way explicitly into Ovid's poetry in *Ars* 1.175, where, in the context of listing places where you might meet girls, he invokes the Latin pun *orbis in urbe*, 'the whole world is in the city'.

But turning women into a metaphor does not always solve the problem. For instance, the female reader and pupil of *Ars* 3, as many have noted, needs instruction of a rather different kind from her male counterpart. While the male pupil of Books 1 and 2 is being taught to behave in ways that will get him what he wants, she must refashion herself into a passive object of his desire, thereby (at least implicitly) doing most of his job for him. Instructions to the male lover about his physical appearance are straightforward: avoid body odour and clip your nose hair; anything more is foppish. Women, by contrast, receive nearly three hundred lines of detailed instruction about what is likely to be wrong with their looks (*Ars* 3.100–280). The teacher here seeks to make women complicit in their own oppression, showing them that they are fundamentally flawed. The women of the *Heroides* are also plausibly seen as victims of a will to power, especially those who are left by a man with grand ambitions. Aeneas is the most obvious, but quite a number of the heroines suggest that the men to whom they write are sacrificing a chance at real love for a selfish, self-imposed duty.

In spite of their tribulations and enforced passivity, however, women's sufferings are often described with apparent sympathy. For some, this is in fact *the* problem with Ovid's poetry: is the poetic persona really sympathetic to women/victims, or is it rather that he relishes the details of their suffering? (There are a number of moments in Ovid's poetry which are too vivid for many readers in their luxuriant description of violence, like the description of Philomela's cut-out tongue.) To put the issue somewhat differently, why must there be *so many* suffering women in Ovid?

The question is not really answerable in this form. But we might put it into the larger context of status-based relationships as a whole. For male upper-class Roman citizens (which category includes both Ovid himself and the majority of his readership, at least aspirationally), the world will have been full of inferiors: women, slaves, children, barbarians and the *plebs*, that great mass of urban poor (also rural poor, but these were not living in Rome). Equals will have been few in number, superiors still fewer. But it has been convincingly argued that one of the main wellsprings of elegy is precisely elite males' anxiety about the erosion of their own power, most particularly with the gradual but unmistakable encroachment of Augustus into more and more aspects of life. As we noted earlier (see Section 1.2), the senatorial and equestrian classes found themselves with fewer and fewer of the traditional avenues toward advancement and honour, and they may or may not have been interested in taking advantage of new opportunities. So some of Ovid's near-obsession with working out who really has the power, and how badly they will abuse it, may come from the distressing elements of contemporary life.

While Ovid's engagement with female victimization is certainly considerable, gender is but one lens through which he treats the topic of power differentials. For most human societies, sex is a fundamental distinguishing characteristic: it is more basic – because more permanent – than such attributes as class or religion or politics; more familiar – because more frequently encountered in daily life, even in the metropolis of Rome – than such attributes as race or ethnicity. From the moment of a child's birth, it is assigned a gender, which brings with it specific, culturally determined, opportunities and limitations. Devoting so much of his poetic attention to relationships between the sexes allowed Ovid also to think through other kinds of difference in an implicit way. This is certainly not to underplay the reality of women's suffering in his poems – quite the contrary: it suggests that these figures have a more personal significance to Ovid himself than it might at first seem, and so offers us a way of seeing him not simply as a man who likes women to be hurt, but as expressing solidarity with victims of all kinds.

In slaveholding societies such as Rome, one's status vis à vis freedom is also a primary means of differentiation. This issue is complicated by the fact that Romans regularly freed their slaves, and provided freed slaves with gradations of access to the privileges of the free (for instance, freed slaves could become Roman citizens, but could not hold public office; their freeborn children, however, could). Beyond this, Roman comedies and schoolboy exercises are full of stories about children being kidnapped by pirates and sold into slavery, which reflects the life experiences of some Romans. So civic status is a category of difference which has less permeable boundaries than sex, and this relative fluidity may be one of the features that render it a disturbing one. Some of Ovid's stories about men who become women and vice versa can interestingly be interpreted as obliquely referring to the tension caused by those who change status from free to slave, and slave to free. But the poetry is also full of literal slaves and freedpersons: in addition to Cypassis from *Am.* 2.7–8, Ovid also has dealings with the slave Nape in *Am.* 1.11, the eunuch doorkeeper Bagoas in *Am.* 2.2–3 and the freed gladiator in *Am.* 3.8, and he provides advice about the tricky question of how to handle, and especially whether one should rape/seduce, the female slaves of the *puella* at *Ars* 1.351–98. Here too, it is not wholly obvious where the poet's sympathies lie.

Nationality is a further category of identity which does not always bring with it strong differentiating potential (although those born in wealthy countries are always more likely to live longer and more prosperous lives than those born in poor countries). As with freed slaves, Rome did have the capacity for integrating foreigners, usually also over several generations – and in fact, many other peoples first encountered the Romans in warfare, becoming captive slaves who eventually became 'Roman' (in spite of also being Greek, Gallic, German, Syrian or any one of dozens of other nations conquered by the Romans). The eunuch Bagoas from *Amores* 2.2 and 2.3 (almost certainly foreign) is for Ovid little more than a stereotype, but he provides a telling example: the first poem entreats him to open the door, reasoning with him 'man to man' about his own advantage; the second turns on him, sneering at his inability to know 'true love' and putting him in his (lowly) place.

Indeed, we have already observed that the compassion with which Ovid's poetry tells the stories of and sometimes even commiserates with various individuals who are victimized, is only part of the story of his interest in power and difference. It is often also the case that, as with Bagoas, Ovid abruptly switches tactics. Think again of Philomela's gory tongue, the description of which forces our complicity: the fact that we are willing to keep reading implies that we are the kind of reader who likes stories about violence perpetrated upon others, or, at the least, that we will put up with them. In effect, then, we have bought into the poetic persona's characterization of the world as divided into abusers and victims, and have perhaps also put ourselves into one of the categories.

Victims into Villains

This subtle but powerful implication of the reader happens on a larger scale as well. Traditional elegy, in fact, is predicated upon the notion of this sort of reversal, with its invocation of the 'slavery of love' which depicts the (slave-owning, wealthy) lover as in thrall to his (lower class, probably prostitute) *puella*, begging for her favours along with a host of other rivals. Yet the elegiac pose of powerlessness, as we have already seen, is easily shed when the opportunity to exploit others presents itself. The *Ars* too, which presents itself as offering help to men who do not know how to fall in love, begins innocently enough. But before the first book is over, would-be lovers are advised to rape the *puella*, who actually wants them to: 'when she, who might have been forced, goes off untouched, however much she pretends joy on her face, she will be sad', *Ars* 1.677–8.

One of the more interesting features of Ovid's victims is precisely the fact that some of them mimic the poet's persona in turning into perpetrators of violence after they suffer it. We have already seen, in the figure of Medea in *Her.* 12 (see Section 3.1), how quickly a wronged woman can turn nasty. And the story of Philomela's rape and silencing continues: once Tereus cuts out her tongue, aroused by the new spectacle, he 'is said to have often sought out her mangled body again for his lust' (*Met.* 6.562). Tereus, of course, is a barbarian, from Thrace; we might not expect anything better of him (although it is not impossible to imagine the narrator of the *Amores* or the *Ars*, in an angry moment, contemplating such a violent act). Tereus then imprisons Philomela in a shed in the woods. She weaves her story on to a tapestry, which she manages to send to her sister Procne, who rescues her. The two women return to Procne's home, kill her son, cook him, and serve him to his father Tereus. Father eats son, the women gloat, and, as Tereus rises up in violence, all are turned into different birds (the women mourning, the man predatory). Ovid's point might be that women are more savage than men (though it is perhaps difficult for us to evaluate whose crime is worse, the narrator plumps for infanticide and cannibalism over rape and dismemberment and more rape). And we can find hints of such a 'moral to the story' elsewhere in the *Metamorphoses*. Perhaps the most interesting aspect of this compelling tale, however, is that the narrator is content simply to drop the story rather than offering an explicit lesson: the real moral may simply be that cruelty inevitably begets more cruelty, or that human beings sometimes do dreadful things to one another.

The story of Daedalus is also interesting in this respect; in fact, he brings together a number of important Ovidian themes. He is another great artist figure, treated in *Ars* 2 and *Met.* 8: enslaved by Minos and imprisoned on Crete, he builds the famous labyrinth to house the Minotaur (an artefact some have seen as metaphorical for the poem itself, especially as it occurs in its dead centre; we readers have managed to get in, but can we get out again?). Eventually, he escapes his prison, on wings he has fashioned for himself out of feathers, wax and twine. He also makes a pair for his son, Icarus, and instructs him in their use: flying too high will melt the wax, and flying too low will drench the wings. Daedalus himself is successful, but Icarus is not. In his sheer joy at being able to fly, he goes too high, and ends up drowned, in what becomes the Icarian Sea. Icarus has been read for hundreds of years as the poster child of over-ambitiousness; indeed, Daedalus's twinned speeches to him can also be read as literary manifestoes to keep to the 'middle way' rather than aiming at an overwrought or a vulgar style.

Daedalus's tale appears somewhat optimistic: a talented artist manages, at great personal cost, to escape from captivity through his own genius. We might even read the story metaphorically, noting that his loss of a son is compensated for in some way by his marvellous creations. But here too, as with Tereus, Philomela and Procne, there is a sting in the tail: as Daedalus buries his son, a partridge looks on, 'demonstrating its joy by a song' (*Met.* 8.238). This partridge was once Daedalus's nephew, apprenticed to the great man. Indeed, his gifts might even have surpassed those of his teacher, for while still in childhood he invented the saw and the compass. The jealous Daedalus threw his nephew off a cliff (he was changed into the ground-loving partridge by Minerva, who favours inventive types). So Daedalus, in retrospect, is difficult to cast as a suffering father; perhaps instead he has been punished, in some cosmic way, for the life he took.

In poetry, as in life, we rarely get the 'whole' story. So one message to derive from Ovid's focus on those who abuse power may be that life isn't fair. Another may be that it *is*, that committing violence and coercing others brings its own cost. This insight can also be applied to the exile poetry, with some surprising results. The fact that Ovid sustains the stance of a victim fairly consistently in his poems from Tomis (only occasionally does rage break out, marring his submissive pose) can be understood as the natural, inevitable result of what he views as the power exercised upon him. It is easy to assume that this time, in real life, Ovid has suffered an arbitrary force. But we cannot know for sure, without knowing whether his punishment was deserved. It *looks* like Ovid has no means of getting revenge, and that he is permanently among the class of victims. Yet the exile poetry never ceases to comment upon Augustus, sometimes justifying his behaviour, sometimes questioning it: either way, the enquiry remains open.

If Ovid's implicit portrait of the world – which allows for only victims and perpetrators – is accurate, one might well choose to be a perpetrator. But for most people this would not happen without some residue of guilty feeling. And, of course, the choice is not always available, such that a Roman with limited power, like Ovid, might move between noticing the ways in which he has progressively lost cherished privileges, unconsciously causing suffering to those with less power, resolving to accumulate greater power, commiserating with others in a similar case, and occasionally deliberately exploiting others. It is not clear that this is an accurate model of human relationships, but it is one which seems prevalent in contemporary Roman authors. Ovid's own explorations of the problem do not provide a solution, but they show that it engaged him throughout his life.

3.3 Empire and Colonialism

We have already noticed a number of the characteristics of the world into which Ovid was born, and how they show themselves in his poetry. This final section treats more explicitly the disjunction between Ovid's status as a high-ranking Roman citizen and the various borders and margins he places, or finds, himself at. We also re-engage with the question of whether it makes sense to see Ovid as 'pro-Augustan', 'anti-Augustan', or occupying some other position in relation to the emperor.

Ovid's poetry often locates itself at the margins: the poet's own persona, and many of his characters, are outsiders looking in, whether the exile seeking a new home, the lover seeking a *puella*, or the victim scar(r)ed into silence. And yet, what feels 'outside' to one person can seem to another like quite a central location. Ovid is often seen as a rebel speaking truth to power, a political martyr pointing out losses of freedom and imperial injustices. We shall look more closely into the specifically political aspects of Ovid's poetry, but let us first notice the less obvious ways in which it displays its complicity in the Roman worldview, which presumes that there are winners and losers, masters and slaves, conquerors and conquered (see too Section 3.2 on Ovid's interest in narratives of victimization, which do not always ally themselves with the victims).

For one thing, Ovid's readers are encouraged to enjoy the fruits of empire, but not to think too much about how they are produced; primary among these fruits is the wide variety of seducible women which cosmopolitan Rome provides (see Section 1.2). Elsewhere Ovid notes that Corinna's (self-inflicted) baldness can be remedied by the purchase of hair from captive German women (*Am.* 1.14.45–50). And despite the elegist's insistence that he is a lover, not a fighter, he has shown himself profoundly interested in dominance; the enslavement of others literally enables the elegiac lifestyle to continue. The soldier, maligned in Ovid's love-poetry, is in fact a shadow-self, doing the dirty work that enables him to occupy the position of victor enjoying the spoils. The creams and ointments of the *Medicamina Facei Femina* similarly rely upon the availability of a variety of non-native substances, and the *Ars* casually refers to jewels brought from abroad (1.251–2, 3.129). More subtly, Ovid's poem on the death of Corinna's parrot, 'a gift provided by the other side of the world' (*Am.* 2.6.38), erases the violence and subjugation necessary to bring exotic luxury goods to Rome (we might view the parrot as a prisoner of war, forced to entertain

the *puella* for his supper: even poetry is forced to serve those in power).
Ovid sometimes bemoans the current age, which ruins the simpler
times of the past with its focus on wealth (*Fas.* 1.337–49), but the
assurance that the modern age suits him best is much more characteristic
(*Ars* 3.121).

It is also relevant to note here that, even in exile, Ovid is a profoundly
Roman poet. We have seen the ways in which he shares the Roman
worldview; beyond this, much of his poetry makes sense only in the
context of urban Rome, a statement which is true of elegy as a whole.
This is sometimes explicit, as in *Ars* 1.69–72, where the instructor gives
advice about where to find women: his list, an erotic topography of the
city, includes the porticoes of Octavia (Augustus's sister) and Livia (his
wife), and shows that the *Ars* unreflectively presumes a Roman
readership. Rome, according to Ovid, is 'locus of empire, and the gods'
(*Tr.* 1.5.70).

Outside of elegy, the situation remains the same. The *Metamorphoses*
covers more or less the entire civilized world, from exotic east to Greece
to Rome itself – but it does so in a teleological way, implying that
Rome is the culmination of all that has gone before. The only parts
of the world left out of the *Metamorphoses*, in fact, are the barbaric
fringes, especially in the north, places where the empire has not
permeated. So once again, *orbis in urbe*, the whole world is contained
within the remit of Rome (see Section 3.2). Later in life, of course,
Ovid has ample opportunity to explore and document one of these only
partly Romanized hinterlands, and his attitude toward it is thoroughly
Roman: disdainful, supercilious and faintly disgusted, the unwitting
colonizer documents just how badly the northern savages need Rome's
civilizing influence (this is a theme of many poems; see especially
EP 1.2 and 4.13, the latter of which describes a Getic poem Ovid claims
to have written, furthering the work of colonization by instructing
the barbarians in Augustus's deification). And Ovid does some of that
work, depicting the 'barbarians' as increasingly humanized – perhaps
through his good example. In the process, he also makes clear that
Rome is, for him, the only place worth living: among many examples,

see *Tr.* 1.3, 3.1, 3.8, 3.12 (about the spring, such as it is, in Tomis), *EP* 1.8, 4.4 and 4.9.

Among the many aspects of Ovid's exile poetry that scholars have found puzzling, the poems in which the poet imaginatively recreates Roman triumphs (a sort of military parade, increasingly restricted to members of the emperor's own family) are paramount. Ovid has not actually seen these events, however much they resemble one another due to their ritualized format – and, in fact, one of the occasions he describes never actually occurred. This is also true of Ovid's pre-exilic foray into the triumph-poem, an excursus at *Ars* 1.177–218 predicting a Parthian triumph for Gaius Caesar, who dies before he can win the victory. The Gaius passage suggests a patriotic, perhaps even jingoistic, side to the poet which is hard to find elsewhere, but surely present in moments like the end of the *Metamorphoses*, which speaks of Rome's glory. But Ovid's tongue-in-cheek description of himself, led in a triumph of the god Cupid in *Am.* 1.2, ought to make it more difficult to take his later triumph entirely seriously. Some scholars see in the *Epistulae Ex Ponto* in particular the seeds of later Latin panegyric, and laud the poet for innovating here as well, offering a first answer to the difficult question of how you discuss the emperor without either getting in trouble or selling out. We might see them as evidence of Ovid's willingness to explore any likely avenue to show himself a good Roman, or we might find troubling indications of the same old Ovid.

This returns us to politics: the question of what Ovid really thought of Augustus (or, for that matter, what Augustus really thought of Ovid) is not one we are in a position to answer. What we can say, however, is that the exile poetry, in continuity with the poet's pre-exilic oeuvre, displays a fundamental ambiguity on the issues. Some readers point to the explicit praises of the imperial family in the exile poetry; others find in them subversive or ironic elements. Still others avoid the question, either by suggesting that Ovid was never interested in politics (and so innocent of any pointed intent, taken unaware by the notion that poetry could have anything to do with life), or by observing that there was no feasible alternative to Augustus (and so, presumably, no such thing as genuine 'anti-Augustanism', no platform for Ovid to be espousing). Both positions oversimplify a bit, but the second is a more defensible claim than the first: we know from anecdotes about dramatic performances that Romans were ready to see allusions to current events even in lines written before they were born, and so it is naïve to suggest that when Ovid refers to Augustus as 'Jupiter', he never expects readers to wonder if Augustus is only the ruler, or also the rapist (see Section 2.1).

Additional difficulty is provided by the fact that moderns are suspicious of panegyric (we live in an age of cynicism, uncomfortable with sentiment). In this view, all praise is tainted with insincerity and coercion, all imperial subjects dissatisfied but too frightened to protest – a position which indicts the majority of Latin literature of hypocrisy (and which, incidentally, has spawned a series of fascinating fictional works on Ovid). The temptation is therefore great either to see Ovid as subversively continuing to thumb his nose at Augustus, or to view him as having caved in to pressure, and having turned to propaganda. There is almost no passage in Ovid which refers to contemporary events which could not be understood in more than one way. For instance, the *Fasti* contains a lengthy entry on the Ides of March, the date on which Augustus's adoptive father Caesar was assassinated. Ovid could have proclaimed sympathy for the self-styled Liberators, or he might have bemoaned the crime. But this is too crude: instead, the narrator offers 150 lines (3.523–696) about Anna Perenna, Dido's sister, exiled and eventually making her way to Latium, but fleeing when Aeneas's jealous wife Lavinia plots to kill her. He offers four possible etymologies of the name of the goddess, whose holiday was a favourite with the common people, but is able to settle upon none. Only then does he admit that he was not planning to mention the death of Caesar, except that Vesta, goddess of the hearth, appeared and insisted (Caesar was her priest). She asserts that she saved Caesar's body from the swords; it was only his shadow that was harmed. And the passage concludes with mention of Caesar's translation into the heavens, his temple, and the statement that those who dared such an unspeakable thing (*nefas*, the opposite of the <u>Fas</u>-*ti*'s subject matter) are all dead by the hand of Augustus (a similar story is told by Venus in *Met.* 15, but with some interesting differences).

Perhaps the single most interesting aspect of this rich passage is that it is not clear where Vesta stops speaking and the narrator takes over – in whose voice precisely is it a *nefas*? And why does Caesar take second place to Anna Perenna? The situation is just the same with other dates in the *Fasti* which might provoke interest from an Augustan point of view. Some scholarship suggests that the *Fasti* was Ovid's earnest, but bungled, attempt to placate the angry emperor, but other readers are less certain, seeing in the poem the same narrative tactics of engagement and withdrawal, of unexpected expansion and compression, as are prevalent in the *Metamorphoses*. Even the fact that the *Fasti* is only half-complete, stopping just before July and August, months in which something would have to be said about Augustus and his adoptive father, can be pinned down to no single explanation. We might conclude that exile precluded further researches, or that Ovid found the topic uncongenial. Or we might imagine that Ovid was holding the second half of the year hostage until Augustus allowed him to return home, or that he tried to write about Augustus's month but could not stomach it, or even that his study in Tomis was littered with drafts which simply never made it into the manuscript tradition.

Given, then, that Ovid seems to be quite capable of frustrating our desire for a clear answer on any point, we might do better to take a wider view, considering praise of emperors to be a neutral feature of imperial Latin literature, without attacking or defending individual passages. When we do look at Ovid's poetry from exile – *Tr.* 2, his 'open letter' to Augustus, is an excellent, because the most sustained, example – we must remember that we are hearing only one side of the story. There, Ovid suggests that the emperor may not have read the *Ars*; he is so busy, and it is so frivolous. Of course, if that is true, then Augustus had no business judging him. Or perhaps he has read it: he is then a sophisticated enough reader to know that literature cannot really affect behaviour (or perhaps he is not?). By choosing both the medium – poetry – and the charge against which he will offer a defence – poetry – and by portraying

Augustus as an angry and irrational divinity who must be appeased, Ovid creates an airtight case. At the same time, it is only one side of the story: Ovid himself hints us that there is more to it when he refers to his *error*.

While many readers of Ovid will continue to take one side or another of the pro/anti-Augustan debate, and will find ample evidence within the poetry to support either position, this book has sought to situate Ovid within the context of empire, rather than in opposition to it. We have noticed the many ways in which the Roman (or Augustan) imperialistic project maps onto Ovid's own totalizing tendencies and influences his outlook. So while Ovid can be understood as seeking to destabilize the Augustan order, we might also observe that his attempts at sabotage serve rather to confirm its reality, and importance. I have also suggested that Ovid is a creature of his own time, and that his relationship to the state is a symbiotic one. For just as the elegist needs the soldier to define himself against, so too, the politician may need the 'dissident voice' to delimit what is and is not allowed. Of course the *Ars* is a mischievous take on didactic poetry which pokes gentle fun at the *princeps'* belief that he can legislate morality. But at the same time, in its drive to categorize the uncategorizable, and in its constant reliance upon *labor*, the application of effort, it is also a profoundly Augustan cultural product. Each man ultimately intrudes into the sphere of the other: Augustus's incursions into Roman private life (especially Ovid's!) are paralleled by Ovid's own attempts at writing poetry about public issues. And we cannot know who started it.

The End

This brief study offers a starting-place for those beginning to read Ovid. It places him in his context both historically and poetically, and explores a number of themes that run throughout his work as a whole. My more ambitious aim has been to suggest that Ovid is 'good to think with', that his poetry occurs right at the nexus of a number of the most important concerns of the Augustan period – and not coincidentally, our own – and that he involves readers in reflection upon some of the most fruitful and perennial questions that literature can ask. To engage fully with Ovid is to recognize that he is the representative of a particular worldview, rather than simply the author of a group of poems. Indeed, in its suspicion of easy answers, its juxtaposition of playfulness and seriousness, and its willingness to experiment on almost every level, Ovid's is a world not so different from our own. Beyond this, of course, my goal has been to encourage the reading of Ovid himself.

Each generation creates its own Ovid to suit its particular concerns; for many of them, he was a poet of profound insight into the human heart. For some (especially during the Romantic era), he was insincere and frivolous, too superficial to engage with the genuine issues of his time. Some have seen him as a dissident political voice, speaking truth to power; some as concerned solely with aesthetics. The twenty-first century sees many things through an Ovidian lens, whether it knows it or not: it is suspicious of sentiment, but also of logic; it believes in individuals and mistrusts authority; it suspects that power relations underpin everything.

Further Readings

The format of the series in which this book appears necessitates extreme selectivity in secondary sources. The fifty sources below are all written in English (although Ovidians write in many languages), and I have favoured books over articles (so too I have omitted 'companions' and other introductory volumes on Ovid, assuming that they would be easy for readers to locate). As I hope this book has made clear, there are many ways of reading Ovid, some of them mutually contradictory, and I have tried to give some sense of this richness in my bibliographic selections.

The first place to go for more information on Ovid is, of course, Ovid: those who have read none of the poetry might be best served by starting with the *Metamorphoses*, as it is probably the most accessible; there are many good contemporary translations available of all Ovid's works. Note too that modern commentaries on ancient works are often the best place to find information about specific stories, even for those without Latin; most have very good introductions to the works they treat, and provide resources for further research in their discussions of individual passages. In the lists below, I have placed an asterisk by the single work in each section that I think those new to Ovidian scholarship will find most accessible.

Poetics and Themes

Fränkel, H. (1945), *Ovid: a Poet between Two Worlds* (Sather Lectures vol. 18), Berkeley: University of California Press.

Hardie, Ph. (2002), *Ovid's Poetics of Illusion*, Cambridge: Cambridge University Press.

Hinds, S. (1987), *The Metamorphosis of Persephone: Ovid and the Self-conscious Muse*, Cambridge: Cambridge University Press.

*Hinds, S. (1987), 'Generalising about Ovid', *Ramus* 16: 4–31.

James, S. L. (2003), *Learned Girls and Male Persuasion: Gender and Reading in Roman Love Elegy*, Berkeley: University of California Press.

Johnson, W. R. (1970), 'The Problem of the Counter-Classical Sensibility and Its Critics', *California Studies in Classical Antiquity* 3: 123–51.

Konstan, J. D. (1991), 'The Death of Argus, or What Stories Do: Audience Response in Ancient Fiction and Theory', *Helios* 18: 15–30.

Martelli, F. (2013), *Ovid's Revisions: The Editor as Author*, Cambridge: Cambridge University Press.

Sharrock, A. (1994), *Seduction and Repetition in Ovid's* Ars Amatoria *2*, Oxford: Oxford University Press.

Wyke, M. (2002), *The Roman Mistress: Ancient and Modern Representations*, Oxford: Oxford University Press.

Amores, Heroides, Ars, and *Remedia*

Barchiesi, A. (1993), 'Future Reflexive: Two Modes of Allusion and Ovid's *Heroides*', *Harvard Studies in Classical Philology*: 95, 333–65.

Boyd, B. W. (1997), *Ovid's Literary Loves: Influence and Innovation in the* Amores, Ann Arbor, MI: University of Michigan Press.

Farrell, J. (1998), 'Reading and Writing the *Heroides*', *Harvard Studies in Classical Philology* 94:307–38.

Fulkerson, L. (2005), *The Ovidian Heroine as Author: Reading, Writing, and Community in the* Heroides, Cambridge: Cambridge University Press.

Henderson, J. (1991), (1992), 'Wrapping up the Case: Reading Ovid, *Amores* 2.7 (+8)', *Materiali e Discuzione* 27: 37–88 and 28: 27–83.

Miller, P. A. (2004), *Subjecting Verses: Latin Love Elegy and the Emergence of the Real*, Princeton: Princeton University Press.

*Myerowitz, M. (1985), *Ovid's Games of Love*, Detroit: Wayne State University Press.

Metamorphoses

Ahl, F. M. (1985), *Metaformations: Soundplay and Wordplay in Ovid and Other Classical Poets*, Ithaca, NY: Cornell University Press.

Feldherr, A. (2010), *Playing Gods: Ovid's Metamorphoses and the Politics of Fiction*, Princeton: Princeton University Press.

*Johnson, P. (2008), *Ovid Before Exile: Art and Punishment in the* Metamorphoses, Madison, WI: University of Wisconsin Press.

Keith, A. M. (1992), *The Play of Fictions: Studies in Ovid's* Metamorphoses *Book 2*, Ann Arbor, MI: University of Michigan Press.

Myers, K. S. (1994), *Ovid's Causes: Cosmogony and Aetiology in the* Metamorphoses, Ann Arbor, MI: University of Michigan Press.

Tissol, G. (1997), *The Face of Nature: Wit, Narrative, and Cosmic Origins in Ovid's* Metamorphoses, Princeton: Princeton University Press.

Wheeler, S. M. (1999), *A Discourse of Wonders: Audience and Performance in Ovid's* Metamorphoses, Philadelphia: University of Pennsylvania Press.

Fasti, Tristia and *Epistulae Ex Ponto*

Barchiesi, A. (1997), *The Poet and the Prince: Ovid and Augustan Discourse*, Berkeley: University of California Press.

Casali, S. (1997), '*Quaerenti plura legendum*: on the necessity of "reading more" in Ovid's exile poetry', *Ramus* 26.1: 80–112.

*Gibson, B. (1999), 'Ovid on Reading: Reading Ovid. Reception in Ovid *Tristia* II', *Journal of Roman Studies* 89: 19–37.

Hejduk, J. (2014), *The Offense of Love*, Madison, WI: University of Wisconsin Press, pp. 30–40 on 'Ovid's Exile: Fact and Fiction'.

McGowan, M. (2009), *Ovid in Exile: Power and Poetic Redress in the* Tristia *and* Epistulae Ex Ponto, Leiden: Brill.

Newlands, C. E. (1995), *Playing with Time: Ovid and the* Fasti, Ithaca, NY: Cornell University Press.

Williams, G. D. (1994), *Banished Voices: Readings in Ovid's Exile Poetry*, Cambridge: Cambridge University Press.

Ovidian Reception

Allen, P. L. (1992), *The Art of Love: Amatory Fiction from Ovid to the Romance of the Rose*, Philadelphia: University of Pennsylvania Press.

Barkan, L. (1986), *The Gods Made Flesh: Metamorphosis and the Pursuit of Paganism,* New Haven: Yale University Press.

Bate, J. (1993), *Shakespeare and Ovid*, Oxford: Oxford University Press.

Clark, J., Coulson, F. T. and McKinley, K. L. (eds.) (2011), *Ovid in the Middle Ages*, Cambridge: Cambridge University Press.

Hofmann, M. and Lasdun, J. (1995), *After Ovid: New Metamorphoses,* New York: Farrar, Straus and Giroux.

*Hughes, T. (1997), *Tales from Ovid,* New York: Farrar, Straus and Giroux.

Ingleheart, J. (ed.) (2011), *Two Thousand Years of Solitude: Exile After Ovid,* Oxford: Oxford University Press.

Martindale, Ch. (1988), *Ovid Renewed: Ovidian Influences on Literature and Art from the Middle Ages to the Twentieth Century,* Cambridge: Cambridge University Press.

Stapleton, M. L. (1996), *Harmful Eloquence: Ovid's Amores from Antiquity to Shakespeare,* Ann Arbor, MI: University of Michigan Press.

Ziolkowski, Th. (2005), *Ovid and the Moderns,* Ithaca, NY: Cornell University Press.

Augustan Context

*Fear, T. (2000), 'The Poet as Pimp: Elegiac Seduction in the Time of Augustus', *Arethusa* 33: 217–39.

Feeney, D. C. (2007), *Caesar's Calendar: Ancient Time and the Beginnings of History,* Berkeley: University of California Press.

Galinsky, G. K. (1996), *Augustan Culture: an Interpretive Introduction,* Princeton: Princeton University Press.

Habinek, T. N. (1998), *The Politics of Latin Literature: Writing, Identity, and Empire in Ancient Rome,* Princeton: Princeton University Press (esp. the chapter on Ovid's exile poetry).

Milnor, K. (2005), *Gender, Domesticity, and the Age of Augustus: Inventing Private Life,* Oxford: Oxford University Press.

O'Gorman, E. (1997), 'Love and the Family: Augustus and Ovidian Elegy', *Arethusa* 30: 103–23.

Powell, A. (ed.) (1992) *Roman Poetry and Propaganda in the Age of Augustus,* London: Bristol Classical Press (esp. Feeney, 1–25 and Kennedy, 26–58).

Raaflaub, K. A. and Toher, M. (eds.) (1990), *Between Republic and Empire: Interpretations of Augustus and his Principate,* Berkeley: University of California Press (esp. Nugent, 239–57).

Glossary of Proper Names and Latin Terms

Achelous river-god.

Actaeon hunter who accidentally saw the goddess Diana bathing; furious, she turned him into a stag and he was gored by his own dogs.

Actium a battle, fought in Greece on 2 September 31 BCE between Octavian and Antony (and Cleopatra), which marked the end of the Antonine faction, and so is often seen as a starting date for the Roman Empire.

Aeneas Trojan refugee and one of the mythical founders of Rome; his story is told (most famously) by Vergil in the *Aeneid*.

Ajax the second-strongest Greek in the Trojan War, after Achilles. He was eventually humiliated and committed suicide.

Althaea decided to take revenge on her son Meleager for killing her brothers; his life was linked to a log that was burning in the fireplace when he was born, so she threw it back onto the fire.

Andromeda Ethiopian princess who was supposed to be sacrificed to a sea monster, but was rescued by Perseus, who then married her.

Anna Perenna Carthaginian sister of Dido who sought help from Aeneas in Italy, but did not receive it; a very popular festival at Rome celebrated her.

Arachne mortal woman weaver who challenged Athena to a contest, and as a result was turned into a spider (hence arachnids).

Aratus Greek poet of the Hellenistic period, who wrote a *Phainomena* ('Appearances'), about the constellations; his work was very influential on poets of Ovid's day.

Argos the hundred-eyed watcher of Io; after Mercury killed him, Juno turned him into the peacock, which has many eye-like decorations on its feathers.

Ariadne mythic woman who helped Theseus find his way out of the Minotaur's labyrinth. She left Crete with Theseus, but was abandoned by him and eventually rescued by Bacchus.

Athena virgin goddess of wisdom, warfare (especially strategy) and the arts. She protected quite a number of heroes, but also persecuted some.

Augustus = Octavian, first Roman emperor, r. 27 BCE until his death in 14 CE; brought about a (self-styled) return to the virtues of the past. The

name was voted to him by the Senate in 27 BCE as an honorific title
('revered one').

Bagoas character in the *Amores*, a eunuch whose job was to protect Corinna
from intruders (like Ovid).

Briseis woman captured by the Greeks in the Trojan War and given to
Achilles as a war-prize. She was later commandeered by Agamemnon to
replace his lost woman, which led to an argument between the two men,
and to Homer's *Iliad*.

Cadmus mythic founder of Thebes and exile from Phoenicia.

Callimachus Greek poet of the Hellenistic period, who wrote a number of
works, including the *Aetia* ('Causes'), about the origins of various customs
and things; he is one of the most influential sources for Latin poets.

Callisto daughter of Lycaon, she was one of the attendants of Diana, until she
was raped by Jupiter disguised as Diana. Diana turned her into a bear
(perhaps accidentally), and she eventually became part of the constellation
Ursa Major and Ursa Minor.

Calypso goddess and sorceress who hosted Odysseus for seven years on his
way home from the Trojan War.

Carmen Latin, 'song' or 'poem'.

Catullus a Latin poet of the generation before Ovid; he wrote love poetry
which prefigures Roman elegy.

Clytie nymph who was in love with Helios (the sun god), but whose jealousy
made him angry, such that she became a sunflower.

Corinna Ovid's girlfriend in the *Amores*.

Creusa wife of Aeneas; she fled Troy with him but got lost along the way.

Cypassis a slave/maid of Corinna, Ovid's girlfriend, whom Ovid (eventually)
admitted to having had an affair with.

Daedalus inventive human who built the labyrinth for the Minotaur,
and fashioned wings for himself and his son to escape from their Cretan
prison.

Daphne nymph who had sworn eternal virginity; she was pursued by Apollo
and, in order to avoid rape, prayed to be saved. She was changed into a bay-
tree (= Daphne in Greek).

Demeter goddess of human and, especially, agricultural fertility.

Deucalion half of the only remaining couple after Jupiter destroyed the world
in a flood; he and Pyrrha repopulated the earth by throwing stones, which
turned into human beings.

Diana goddess of the hunt and virginity. She defended her own chastity rigorously, and punished any female or male followers who did not do the same.

Dido Queen of Carthage, she had an ill-fated affair with Aeneas, which eventually led to her suicide; she swore eternal enmity between her people and Aeneas' (which was the ultimate cause of the Punic Wars Rome fought with Carthage over the third and second centuries BCE).

Echo talkative Greek nymph who was prevented from initiating conversations. After falling in love with Narcissus, and responding to his speech, she eventually melted away and now remains only as a sound.

Error Latin, 'mistake', sometimes implying fault and sometimes not.

Euripides one of the trinity of fifth century BCE Greek tragic playwrights (the others being Aeschylus and Sophocles); he is the most similar to Ovid in terms of plot and style.

Evander early mythic hero of Italy, who settled there when exiled from Greece.

Gaius Caesar grandson and adoptive son of Augustus, his early death foiled imperial succession plans.

Helen the most beautiful woman in the world, ever. She was initially married to the Greek Menelaus (brother of Agamemnon), but was taken to Troy by Paris; the Trojan War occurred because the Greeks came to get her back.

Hermione daughter of Helen and Menelaus, married to Neoptolemus (son of Achilles) and then to Orestes, her cousin.

Icarus son of Daedalus, he flew too high and was drowned in the Icarian Sea.

Io raped by Jupiter and then turned into a cow. She was then driven mad, and wandered to Egypt, where she was eventually turned back into a human.

Iphigeneia daughter of Agamemnon and Clytemnestra, she was supposed to be sacrificed to Diana in order to allow the Greeks to go to Troy but according to most versions was spirited away instead; she went to Tauris and was later reunited with her brother Orestes.

Janus god of beginnings (= January); he has a speaking role in Ovid's *Fasti*.

Jason leader of the Argonauts, who went to Colchis to take the Golden Fleece. He was helped by Medea, whom he brought to Greece, but when he later tried to marry someone else, she took a violent revenge.

Julius Caesar one of the warlords of the late Republic; he adopted his relative Octavian (later Augustus), which gave the latter the resources to be able to continue consolidating power. Caesar was assassinated on the Ides of March (15 March 44 BCE).

Juno wife of Jupiter, patron of marriage. She is, especially in Latin poetry, often portrayed as jealous about her husband's repeated affairs.

Lara talkative Italian nymph, raped by Mercury and impregnated.

Livia wife of Augustus, and so first Roman empress, 58 BCE–29 CE.

Lucretius Latin poet writing in the generation before Ovid; his only extant work is the *De Rerum Natura* (= 'on the Nature of Things'), a philosophical and scientific poem about the universe.

Lycaon man who attempted to trick Jupiter during the latter's inspection of the earth; he was turned into a wolf as a punishment for his bloodthirsty deeds.

Marsyas gifted flute-player who challenged Apollo to a musical contest and lost; he was flayed alive.

Medea powerful sorceress from the 'barbarian' east; fell in love with the hero Jason and helped him. Her most (in)famous act is the killing of her own children; she features in many Greek and Roman poems (the most famous of them is Euripides's play *Medea*).

Medusa the Gorgon, whose gaze turned men to stone; she was beheaded by Perseus, but her head retained its properties.

Myrrha daughter who fell in love and had an incestuous relationship with her father. She became pregnant and prayed not to pollute the earth any longer, so was changed into the myrrh tree.

Narcissus beautiful young man who was invulnerable to the charms of anyone but himself; he caught sight of his own reflection and wasted away from desire.

Naso *cognomen* (the third of the Roman 'three names') of Ovid, meaning 'nose'. These seem to have once been nicknames, but soon became hereditary, and denoted branches of larger family groupings.

Nicander Greek poet of the Hellenistic period, who wrote a *Theriaca* ('Wild Things'), about animals whose bite injects venom and an *Alexipharmaca* ('Warding-off Remedies'), about antidotes; his work was very influential on poets of Ovid's day.

Niobe mortal woman with twelve children who thought that she was therefore superior to Leto, mother of Apollo and Diana. Her children were all killed and she turned to stone.

Ocyrhoe female centaur who had the gift of prophecy; she said too much and was turned into a horse.

Odysseus hero of the Trojan War, and the only one of the Greek soldiers to have made it home afterward (Homer's *Odyssey* details his journey).

Orestes son of Agamemnon and Clytemnestra; after his mother killed his father he took vengeance by killing her, and was eventually vindicated.

Orpheus son of the Muse Calliope, and a hero with great musical talent. His wife Eurydice died and he sang a song to persuade the gods of the underworld to allow her to live again, but broke the taboo against looking at her, so lost her a second time.

Pan rustic god who spent much of his time playing music on reed pipes and chasing after nymphs.

Paris son of the Trojan king Priam; he judged the beauty contest of the three goddesses Juno, Minerva and Venus, awarding the prize to Venus, who gave him the Greek Helen in return. This was the ultimate cause of the Trojan War.

Pasiphae woman who fell in love with a bull and managed, through artificial means, to become pregnant by him; the result was the half-bull, half-man Minotaur.

Pater patriae Latin, 'father of the fatherland'; honorific title given to Augustus in 2 BCE.

Penelope wife of Odysseus; she waited at home for him for twenty years, but had a few tricks up her sleeve as well.

Persephone daughter of Demeter, she was kidnapped by her uncle Hades and taken to the underworld. Demeter went on strike and eventually negotiated to have Persephone above ground for part of the year (which is when we celebrate summer).

Perseus mythic hero who killed Medusa the Gorgon and travelled the world slaying monsters. He met, fell in love with, and eventually married the princess Andromeda.

Phaethon illegitimate son of Helios (the sun god) who asked his father for a favour. Promised anything, he demanded to drive the chariot of the sun across the sky, with disastrous results to himself and the earth.

Philomela sister of Procne, she was raped by Tereus and had her tongue cut out. She was eventually turned into a bird.

Pierides mortal sisters who lost a contest to the Muses. Also, the Muses themselves, from the place where they won the contest.

Pontus Roman province from the middle first century BCE, located in (modern) Northern Turkey, named after the Black Sea (= *Pontos* in Greek); it includes Colchis, homeland of Medea.

Procne wife of Tereus and sister of Philomela, she exacted a bloody revenge and was eventually turned into a bird.

Propertius a Latin love elegist contemporary with Ovid, and influential upon him.

Puella Latin, 'girl'; the standard term used for the mistress or girlfriend of elegiac poetry. Plural = *puellae*.

Pygmalion gifted sculptor who created the perfect woman and then, with the help of Venus, brought her to life.

Pylades best friend of Orestes; one of the standard examples from mythology of loyalty among friends.

Pyramus lover of Thisbe; believing her to have been killed by a lion, he committed suicide.

Pyrrha half of the only remaining couple after Jupiter destroyed the world in a flood; she and Deucalion repopulated the earth by throwing stones, which turned into human beings.

Pythagoras Greek mathematician and philosopher, most famous for the theorem named after him ($a^2 + b^2 = c^2$), but also known as an advocate for vegetarianism.

Saecular Games held to mark the end of an era (ca. 100 years), involving athletic events, theatrical performances and religious ceremonies.

Syrinx (= Greek 'reed pipes') one of Pan's victims, who escaped being raped by changing into a reed-bed, which Pan harvested and played.

Tereus barbarian king who married Procne, but fell in love with, kidnapped, and repeatedly raped, her sister Philomela. All three were eventually turned into birds.

Thisbe lover of Pyramus; she came upon his dead body and killed herself. The blood from her body stained the mulberry tree (formerly white) red.

Tiberius r. 14–37 CE; stepson and successor of Augustus, so the second Roman emperor.

Tibullus a Latin love elegist contemporary with Ovid, and influential upon him.

Tithonus husband of the goddess Dawn; he was given eternal life but not eternal youth, so eventually turned into a cricket.

Venus goddess of love and sexual desire. She was also, through her son Aeneas, a founder of the Julian line (and so a patron goddess of Julius Caesar and Augustus).

Vergil probably the most famous Roman poet, who wrote in the generation before Ovid. His poems are the *Eclogues,* the *Georgics* and the *Aeneid.*

Vesta goddess of the hearth and domesticity; she had a number of virgins dedicated to her service and also a male priest.

Index

(Entries in **bold** also appear in the Glossary, pp. 93–99)

abortion 7
Accius 48
Achaemenides 50, 61
Achelous 47, 53
Achilles 36, 42–3
Actaeon 2, 36, 68
Actium 4, 19, 21
adultery (*see also* sex, wives, *puella*) 1,
    2, 6, 18, 22–4
Aeneas 42, 43, 50, 59, 63, 75, 84
Aeneid 4, 5, 25, 43, 49–50
Agamemnon 42
Ajax 36
Althaea 35
ambiguity 2, 5, 11, 16, 19, 25, 27, 38, 45,
    52, 56
Amores 4, 5, 6, 7, 16, 18, 31, 33, 37, 38, 39,
    40, 42, 44, 46, 48, 51, 52, 53, 55, 56,
    57, 61, 64, 73, 74, 76–7, 78, 81, 83
Andromeda 60
Anna Perenna 84–5
Apollo 12, 52, 69, 70
Apollonius 48
Arachne 3, 55–6, 70–2
Aratus 4, 9
Ariadne 63
Ars Amatoria 1, 4, 8, 9, 14, 15, 23–4, 26,
    33, 38, 40, 44, 48, 50, 51, 52, 53,
    56, 57, 59, 61, 74–5, 78, 79, 81, 82,
    83, 85, 86
art, artists 6, 45, 57, 60, 61, 66, 69–72,
    79, 87
Athena (*see* Minerva)
Augustus, Augustanism 1, 2, 3, 4, 9, 11,
    13, 14, 15, 17, 18, 19, 20, 21, 22–4,
    25, 26, 30, 37, 45, 48, 52, 65, 73,
    75, 80, 81, 82, 83–6

Bagoas 76–7
barbarian lands, barbarians 1, 7,
    15, 17, 60, 66, 75, 76–7, 78,
    80–7
biography, autobiography 17, 18, 65,
    68–9, 80
Briseis 42–3, 64

Cadmus 59
Callimachus 14, 40, 48, 49, 53
Callisto 12, 41, 65
Calypso 48
Catullus 17, 30, 31
Chaos, *see* Janus
Chaucer 57
Cicero 49
cinema 32
Clytie 12
Corinna 6, 7, 16, 32, 44, 46, 57, 73, 74,
    81
courtly love 58
Creusa 43
Cupid 31, 32, 33, 37, 83
Cynthia 32
Cypassis 6, 46, 64, 73, 76

Daedalus 79
Dante 58
Daphne 12, 52
dating, Ovidian 3–4
Dawn 39
decorum 35
Deucalion 39
Diana (Artemis) 68, 70
didactic 8, 9, 14, 40, 57, 86
Dido 42, 43, 49, 63, 84
Dylan 57

Echo 57, 67
education (Roman) 35, 36, 76
elegy 7, 8, 9, 11, 16, 18, 24, 27, 29, 30, 33, 38, 42, 44, 47, 51, 70, 73–4, 75, 77, 81, 82, 86
elite (Roman) 17, 20, 22, 24, 35, 75, 80
Ennius 48
epic 5, 9, 11, 29, 30, 31, 32, 33, 38, 47, 52, 64
Epicureanism 8
Epistulae Ex Ponto 2, 4, 15, 25, 30, 47, 49, 62, 82, 83
Equestrian, *see* elite
error (Ovid's) 1, 14, 86
ethnography 15, 17
Euripides 48
Evander 62, 66
Exile, exiles 3, 5, 13, 15, 16, 17, 18, 24, 30, 51, 59–66, 68, 79, 81, 83, 85
exile poetry (Ovid's) 30, 45, 55, 62, 66

Fasti 3, 4, 13, 24, 26, 30, 38, 39, 40, 41, 48, 49, 51, 56, 59, 61, 62, 67, 82, 84–5
feet (metrical) 30–1

Gaius Caesar 83
Gallus 30
genre 4, 7, 11, 16, 19, 26, 31, 33, 42, 47
Georgics 8–9
Germanicus Caesar 9, 25
god (*see also* individual gods) 3, 11, 22, 38, 39, 40, 47, 52, 53, 55, 61, 62, 68, 69, 72, 82, 86
Gorgon, *see* Medusa
Greece, Greeks (also Greek tradition, poetry, etc.) 1, 8, 9, 11, 14, 17, 26, 29, 31, 35, 37, 50, 53, 62, 65, 71, 72, 77, 79, 82

Hebe 41
Helen 8, 56
Hermes 37
Hermione 8, 63

Heroides (single and double) 4, 7–8, 14, 16, 42, 43, 48, 49, 51, 52, 55, 56, 63, 64, 75, 78
Hesiod 49
History 11, 13, 14, 35, 38, 50, 51, 59, 86
Homer 29, 39, 42, 47, 38, 50
Horace 20, 21, 25, 31
humour 14, 15, 18, 35, 36

Ibis 3, 4, 14, 35, 56
Icarus 1, 79
Iliad 42–3
impotence 7, 61
Io 53, 65, 67
Iphigeneia 62
irony 14, 16, 31, 42, 46, 47, 58, 65, 83
Ixion 53

Janus 39, 66
Jason 62, 63–4
Joyce (James) 57
Julia (Augustus' daughter/ granddaughter) 24
Julius Caesar 11, 13, 21, 84–5
Juno 41, 53, 67
Jupiter 14, 37, 41, 53, 65, 67, 84

Lara 67
Lavinia 84
laws (Augustan) 16, 22–4
Lelex 53, 55
Leuconoe/Leucothoe 46
Livia 2, 15, 82
love (*see also* elegy) 8, 14, 31, 32, 36, 40, 51, 52, 58
Lucretius 8, 31, 49
Lycaon 11

Macareus 50, 61
Maecenas 24–5
Malouf 65
marginality/margins 18, 47, 59–66, 67, 72, 80–7

marriage (see also laws) 16, 17, 22–3, 24
Marsyas 69
Medea 4, 8, 29, 42, 48, 49, 55, 59, 62, 63–4, 66, 78
Medicamina Facei Feminae 4, 6, 81
Medusa 60
Mercury 53
Messalla 25
Metamorphoses 3, 4, 6, 8, 9, 11, 12, 13, 16, 20, 26, 29, 32, 33, 34, 35, 36, 38, 41, 42, 46, 47, 49, 50, 51, 52, 53, 55, 59, 61, 63, 64, 66, 67, 68, 69, 70, 71–2, 73, 78, 79, 82, 85
metre 29–31, 32
military matters 16, 19, 24, 30, 33 60–1, 64, 77, 81, 83, 86
Minerva 3, 39, 70–2, 79
Minos 79
Minotaur 79
mortals 37, 39, 40, 41
Mozart 57
Muses 39, 41, 69, 73–4
Myrrha 36, 70
Myrrha 70
Mythology (see also individual characters) 7–8, 11, 13, 14, 35, 38, 39, 43, 51, 56, 63

Naevius 48
Nape 76
Narcissus 36, 67
narrative 6, 11, 12, 31, 38, 39–44, 46, 47, 50, 53, 55, 57, 59, 63, 66, 73, 79, 81, 85, 87
narrative techniques: deception 6, 9
    disequilibrium 33, 38, 40, 44, 45, 46, 47, 87
    incongruity 31, 32, 34, 35–7, 39, 41, 42, 78
Neptune 70
Nicander 8
Niobe 69–70

Octavia 82
Octavian, *see* Augustus
Ocyrhoe 67
Odysseus 11, 36, 47, 48, 50, 55
Orestes 49, 62
Orpheus 61, 69

Pan 53
Paris 41, 56
parody 9, 13, 29, 30, 50
Pasiphae 38
Patronage 24–6, 51
Penelope 49
Persephone 38
Perseus 60–1
persona (see also narrative) 7, 16, 31, 39, 41, 44, 66, 73, 75, 77, 78, 81
Petrarch 58
Phaenomena 4
Phaethon 12, 39, 41
Philomela 34, 65, 67, 75, 77, 78, 79
philosophy 11, 63
Picasso 57
Pierides 69
Pirithous 53, 55
Politics 6, 18–27, 35, 38, 57, 81, 83, 86
power (see also rape, violence) 3, 6–7, 20, 45, 62, 64, 66–80, 84, 87
pregnancy 7
Procne 78, 79
Propertius 20, 25, 30, 32, 48
prostitutes 24, 78
puella 8, 18, 19, 24, 31, 39–40, 44, 45, 50, 56, 57, 58, 70, 73–4, 77, 78, 81
pun 35, 36, 67–8, 74
Pygmalion 70
Pylades 49
Pyramus 33–4
Pyreneus 39
Pyrrha 39
Pythagoras 41, 63

Quintilian 35

Ransmyer 65
Rape (*see also* violence, women) 12,
    23, 41, 52–3, 55–6, 65, 67, 70, 73,
    76–7, 78, 84
Religion, Roman (*see also* gods) 13, 21,
    22, 26, 51, 84
Remedia Amoris 4, 8–9, 40, 51, 52
Repetition 3, 4, 5 42, 47–58, 65, 68–9
rhetoric 35, 36, 47
rivals 40, 44, 78
Rome 1, 7, 11, 13, 17, 18, 19, 20, 21, 22,
    23, 24, 26, 37, 38, 50, 58, 59, 62,
    63, 75, 76, 77, 80–7

senators, *see* elite
Seneca (the elder) 35
Servitium amoris, see slavery
Sex 17, 22–4, 33, 50, 61, 67, 70
Sex changes 76
Shakespeare 34, 58
silence 66–72
Slavery/slavers 6, 7, 33, 59, 64, 75,
    76–8, 81–2
Sophocles 48
stories/storytelling, *see* narrative
Suetonius 24
Sun 12, 39
Syrinx 53

Tereus 34, 67, 78, 79
Theseus 53
Thisbe 34
Tiberius 25, 30, 32, 48
Tithonus 39
Titian 57
Tomis 1, 4, 13, 14, 16, 17, 18, 24, 62, 80,
    83, 85
tragedy 7, 11, 29, 3, 35, 48, 55, 84
Tristia 1, 2, 3, 4, 13, 14, 15, 17, 19, 24,
    30, 45, 47, 49, 51, 62, 68, 82, 83, 85
Trojan War 11, 41, 50
Troy 43

Vegetarianism 63
Venus 37, 70, 85
Vergil 20
Vergil 4, 5, 8–9, 25, 29, 38, 43, 48, 49
Vesta 84–5
victims (*see also* rape, violence) 63,
    72–80, 81
violence (*see also* rape) 3, 34–5, 39–40,
    65, 72–7, 81

war (*see* military matters)
wife/wives 2, 7, 12, 61, 82
Wilde 6
Woman/women 5, 7, 9, 14, 15, 23, 36,
    42–3, 49, 51, 53, 55–6, 57, 61, 70,
    72–7, 78, 81, 82